THE GREEN TEAM

Winning Ideas And Activities
To Promote Environmental Awareness

by
Dorothy Michener

Incentive Publications, Inc.
Nashville, Tennessee

Illustrated by Dianna Richey
Cover by Geoffrey Brittingham
Edited by Leslie Britt

ISBN 0-86530-271-5

TABLE OF CONTENTS

PREFACE

Writing *The Green Team* has required a great deal of information-gathering. I've studied books, pamphlets, brochures, and newsletters, devoured newspaper and magazine articles, talked to kids and teachers, and have been a regular visitor to our local nature conservancy. I have probably amassed enough material for ten books!

The one thing that touched me the most was a few moments alone in the forest. I sat watching one of nature's wonderful spectacles, a waterfall. The raw beauty of that moment tugged at my heart. What will happen to this waterfall, I wondered. What will this place be like in fifty years?

Every child should have one of these marvelous moments that tugs at the heart. The resulting awareness would lead all of us to a commitment to preserving the environment. Baba Dioun, a noted African environmentalist, once wrote:

> *"For in the end, we will conserve only what we love.*
> *We will love what we understand.*
> *We will understand only what we are taught."*

This leaves you, the teacher, with a tremendous responsibility. With *The Green Team* we hope to help you teach your students to understand their world by leading them through a natural progression from appreciation to advocacy. Every page contains an environmental thought, idea, question, or concept for your pupils to ponder. These exercises, along with teacher interaction, will help promote more advanced logical and problem-solving skills. *The Green Team* provides a broad selection of topics and concepts that should fit into your busy schedule, as they include most of the basic skills taught in your classroom. We urge you to modify our ideas so that they will meet student needs, as well as fit in with your own teaching styles. As always, we ask you to adapt and adopt!

Many of the student exercises have been designed for cooperative learning. As you know, team learning is most useful in increasing the motivation of students while helping you to be more effective when handling a diverse group.

Survival is a frightening word. While realizing the need to face reality, we have tried to avoid including threats and fear in our subject matter. We draw instead on excitement and joy, commitment and responsibility. It is our hope that through encounters with natural forces, we can help kids learn to love the outdoors. The students in your classroom today will be the guardians of our planet tomorrow. They need the right tools and information to protect it. Give them everything you've got!

LEARNING WITH THE HEART

We teachers hope that our students will take a stand and move in a positive direction to help save the Earth. Before they can become active conservationists, however, students need to understand the world around them and learn that how they treat the environment now will certainly affect them later.

In this chapter, we have provided simple activities and worksheets to help children develop a sense of appreciation for the environment. "Take a closer look," we repeat over and over again. The subject matter introduced in this chapter is broad. It is difficult to achieve global understanding in twenty-four pages! You, however, can encourage your young naturalists to thoroughly explore their unique locales and to discover the joys and pleasures nature has to offer. Through individual observation and thinking, shared experiences, and team learning we hope to foster in children a greater awareness of the environment.

Most of today's adult role models function "on the run" in business or corporate environments. It's now time dust off the old cliché "take time to smell the flowers" and teach children to tune in to their world with all five senses. As Henry David Thoreau once said, "It is the marriage of the soul with nature that gives birth to the imagination."

LEARNING WITH THE HEART

HIAWATHA'S BROTHERS

"At the door on summer evenings
Sat the little Hiawatha;
Heard the lapping of the water,
Sounds of music, words of wonder..."

Henry Wadsworth Longfellow

In the poem "The Song of Hiawatha" by
Henry Wadsworth Longfellow, a young
Indian boy learns to love the natural
world around him. As your teacher reads
to you about Hiawatha's childhood, make
a list of the things in his environment
that he learns to appreciate.

_____   _____
_____   _____
_____   _____
_____   _____
_____   _____
_____   _____

If the animals in the poem are called Hiawatha's brothers, why do you think
he killed the red deer? _____
_____
_____
_____

More: In your free time, you might want to read more about the legend of
Hiawatha.

Name(s) _____

ENCOUNTER WITH THE LOON

The loon is an elegant yet mysterious bird, sometimes seeming to disappear like a ghost in the water. For more than sixty million years its mournful cry could be heard across the swamps, lakes, and rivers of the world. Loons are divers, plunging deep into the water to feed upon fish and other aquatic life. This trait makes them somewhat difficult for bird watchers to follow.

There are a number of loon species in existence, including the common loon, the red-throated loon, the yellow-billed loon, the Arctic loon, and the Pacific loon. These birds can be found throughout the world, but are most common in the northern hemisphere.

A loon's appearance varies somewhat from breed to breed, but most have a long, pointed bill and dark red eyes. Its dramatic, sometimes checkered, plumage makes the loon easy to spot during the warm months; however, the different species can look quite similar during the winter when their differently colored feathers all turn a dark gray on top and white below.

People have been fascinated with the loon for centuries. Worldwide legends still circulate about loons and their supernatural powers. Their bodies have been found in ancient Indian graves, and in Mongolia some people believed they would be reincarnated as loons. In Siberia loons were once considered sacred and could not be harmed. Even today, some Scandinavian fishermen rely on the loons to help them predict the weather.

The loon still exists in the wild today, although much of its natural habitat is in danger. By understanding these marvelous birds we can hope to protect them from the elements that may some day destroy them.

ENCOUNTER WITH THE LOON

"Do yooo think yooo can dooo this?" asks the Loooon.

After reading about the loon, you should be able to answer the following questions:

1. Why are loons so easy to spot in the summer? _____

_____

2. How do loons feed? _____

_____

3. How many species of loons are there? _____

4. Where do loons help predict the weather? _____

Do some research to answer these questions:

5. What creatures are predators of the loon? _____

_____

6. How do loons communicate? _____

_____

7. Environmental threats to the loon include _____

_____

8. What species of loon, if any, live in your area of the country? _____

_____

9. Why do you think the loon is a survivor? On the back of this sheet, add additional interesting facts you have learned about the loon.

Name(s) _____

ADOPT-A-TREE

Have you ever made friends with a tree? This is your chance to do just that!

Pick out a tree in your school yard, neighborhood, or a nearby park. Watch it carefully in all types of weather and in all seasons. Look at the tree's bark, trunk, and needles or leaves. Touch it, smell it, and listen to the wind blow through its branches.

Take your time! This is a year-long assignment.

1. I named my tree _____

2. The address of my tree is _____
_____

3. My tree is a _____

4. I chose this tree because _____
_____
_____

In autumn my tree looks like
_____
_____
_____
_____

In winter my tree is
_____
_____
_____
_____

In the spring, I see
_____
_____
_____
_____

When summer comes, my tree
_____
_____
_____
_____
_____

On the back of this sheet write the most important things you learned about your friend, the tree.

Name(s)_____

WHO'S HONKING?

GREEN TEAM ASSIGNMENT

Captain _____   **Date** _____

Crew _____   _____

_____   _____

Have you ever watched a "V" of geese flying overhead? Have you ever wondered who decides which goose will be the leader?

If you watch long enough, you will see that every few minutes a different bird moves up to the lead position. It's hard work to be first! The birds that follow the leader are given an aerodynamic lift by the birds up front. Race car drivers and bicyclists call this phenomenon drafting.

A flying squadron of geese is called a skein and is an amazing sight! Often you can hear their musical honking before you can see them. Canadian geese have black heads and long necks with what looks like white chin straps. They are large birds and travel in big groups. These geese can fly as fast as eighty miles per hour at altitudes of three to six thousand feet and can stay aloft for hours at a time.

Canadian geese migrate to parts of the southern United States and Mexico for the winter months. Scientists have found that most birds migrate by day, using rivers and mountains as landmarks. However, some birds use the stars or the Earth's magnetic field to help them fly by night. It would seem that Mother Nature must have her own control tower to guide these geese back home for another summer in the north.

List interesting facts you have learned about the Canadian goose. Use the back of this page if you need more space to write.

1. _____
2. _____
3. _____
4. _____
5. _____

More: As a team, come up with five other questions you have about the Canadian goose. Then, do some research to find out the answers to your questions.

MIRROR, MIRROR

Birds are unique among animals. Why? Birds are the only inhabitants of our planet with feathers. Within a species, a bird is usually classified by its type of beak.

Each of the birds pictured thinks it is very special. Write what you think each one is saying in the voice bubble.

Do you think my beak is too big?

Miss Ostrich says, "

Mr. Parrot says, "

Mrs. Quail says, "

1. Define these words:

   unique _____

   species _____

   classified _____

2. What beautiful birds can be found in your area of the country? _____

   _____

   _____

Name(s) _____

ENVIRONMENTAL "TWO DO'S"

Name _____ Partner _____

"Do One"

Air, land, water, plants, and animals all make up our world's natural environment.
Investigate a mini-environment and see what you can find in it. Do this:

1. Find a partner.
2. Get a piece of string about eighteen inches long. Tie a knot in it.
3. Go outdoors and find a grassy spot.
4. Make a circle with your string. The area within the circle is your mini-environment.
5. Examine the mini-environment carefully. Study it.
6. What do you see? Is there movement?
7. Try another spot if necessary.
8. Make a list on the back of this sheet of what you and your partner find in the mini-environment.
9. Compare your list with those of other students' mini-environments.
10. How is your environment different from the other mini-environments?

Name _____ Partner _____

"Do Two"

1. Find a partner.
2. You will need one cardboard paper towel roll, a pencil, this sheet, and writing paper.
3. Go outdoors and find a quiet spot.
4. Sit down back-to-back with your partner.
5. One person will look through the cardboard roll and find something to look at in the environment.
6. Slowly tell the other person what you see, making sure you describe shapes, colors, sizes, etc.
7. The partner does not look, but writes down what you are dictating.
8. Reverse positions and repeat the process.
9. When you both have finished the activity, look around and try to identify the objects the other has seen.
10. How did you do?

GETTING ANTSY

Do you wonder what life is like for an ant?

The ant is perhaps the most advanced of all insects. Ants live in colonies of up to one thousand, and their society is highly organized. For example, each ant has a designated job: some are builders, others are food gatherers, and some are nurses. Ants are also known for their strength. Have you ever seen an ant carry an object much larger than itself? It is truly fascinating!

Try this:

1. Go outside with a partner. Find a grassy spot.
2. Lie on your back while your partner stands.
3. Pretend you are an ant walking on the ground. Close your eyes and feel slowly along the ground with your fingers.
4. Explore the environment with your fingers.
5. Open your eyes and look at your partner standing above you.
6. Turn your head from one side to the other and look through the grass at an ant's level.
7. Change places with your partner.
8. Try to find some real ants and observe their behavior carefully. Describe their behavior on the back of this sheet.

More: Draw a picture of how you felt as a tiny ant. Write a descriptive sentence under the picture.

Boo!

Name(s)_____

PETER PENGUIN

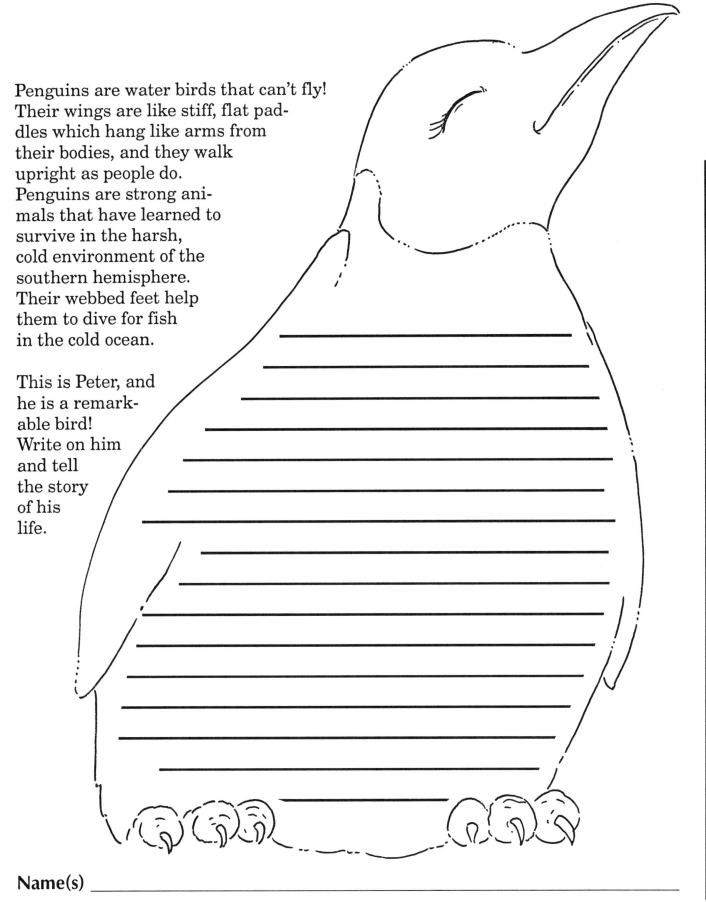

Penguins are water birds that can't fly!
Their wings are like stiff, flat pad-
dles which hang like arms from
their bodies, and they walk
upright as people do.
Penguins are strong ani-
mals that have learned to
survive in the harsh,
cold environment of the
southern hemisphere.
Their webbed feet help
them to dive for fish
in the cold ocean.

This is Peter, and
he is a remark-
able bird!
Write on him
and tell
the story
of his
life.

Name(s) _____

THIS IS FOR THE BIRDS!

When it comes to finding birds outside, your ears can often be more helpful than your eyes. See how many of these types of birds you can find in this puzzle using the clues provided below.

ACROSS

1. Takes babies to the hospital
2. Speedy bird from the cartoons
3. Our United States emblem
4. Proudest bird of all
5. "Stay out of my garden!"
6. Called "ugly" in a fairy tale
7. Tells us it's spring
8. They feast on the highway
9. Found cooing in parks
10. Its wings are like a tiny helicopter

DOWN

1. The Thanksgiving bird
2. Has a huge, silly beak
3. Pink, with long legs and neck
4. Sounds like a meowing cat
5. We love their eggs!
6. Symbol of peace
7. The author Edgar Allen Poe wrote about this black bird
8. Who gives a hoot?
9. This guy doesn't fly
10. "_____" White is the name he calls out

Name(s) _____

©1993 by Incentive Publications, Inc., Nashville, TN.

NATURE SCAVENGER HUNT

It's time for a fun walk! Be a scavenger and see how many things from this list you can spot. Carefully explore the area your teacher takes you to. But remember, be a good conservationist, and don't damage the environment.

Complete this checklist as you go.

CAN YOU FIND?		DESCRIPTION
Feather	√	*long, white with black tip, frayed*
Sand		
Smooth stone		
Moss		
Worm		
Ant		
Caterpillar		
Beetle		
Butterfly		
Spider web		
Spider		
Rabbit		
Seed		
Pod		
Squirrel		
Leaf with points		
Leaf with holes		
Pine needles		
Cactus		
Fungus		
Tumbleweed		
Large animal		
Seedling		

Name(s) _____

©1993 by Incentive Publications, Inc., Nashville, TN.

BLOW, WIND, BLOW!

Although you can't see it, the wind can be wild and wonderful. Learn to estimate wind speed; it can help you to plan your outdoor activities.

CALM
Wind Speed, 0-1 mile per hour
- Lakes, ponds, puddles very still
- No waves at the beach
- Leaves not moving
- Smoke rises straight up

SLIGHT BREEZE
Wind Speed, 2-10 miles per hour
- Leaves rustle
- Ripples on water
- Smoke rises sideways
- Flags move slightly
- Tall grass moves
- Feel breeze on face

MODERATE BREEZE
Wind Speed, 10-20 miles per hour
- Papers blow apart
- Small branches move
- Flags wave
- Small waves on water

STRONG BREEZE
Wind Speed, 20-30 miles per hour
- Small trees sway
- Rain or snow falls sideways
- Dust blows around
- Water has whitecaps
- Hair blows

GALE
Wind Speed, 30-45 miles per hour
- Hard to walk
- Large trees sway
- Branches break
- Large waves on water
- Stay indoors!

Describe the wind speed each day for one week.

Monday _____

Tuesday _____

Wednesday _____

Thursday _____

Friday _____

Saturday _____

Sunday _____

What is your favorite thing to do on a windy day? _____

_____

Name(s)_____

SHORE LIFE/PLAINS LIFE

Some of you may find one half of this page easy and the other half difficult. It all depends on where you live!

Try to match each picture with its correct name.

Shore Life

A
B
C
D
E

1. Horseshoe Crab
2. Sand Dollar
3. Starfish
4. Scallop
5. Mussel
6. Gull
7. Crab
8. Lobster
9. Bass
10. Jellyfish

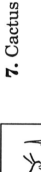

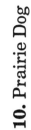

F
G
H
I
J

Plains Life

K
L
M
N
O

1. Jackrabbit
2. Rattlesnake
3. Quail
4. Hawk
5. Tumbleweed
6. Roadrunner
7. Cactus
8. Butte
9. Wheat
10. Prairie Dog

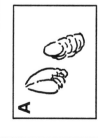

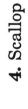

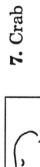

P
Q
R
S
T

More: On the back of this sheet, tell the area in which you would most like to live. Have you ever visited there? Tell about it.

Name(s)

SKY WATCH

Weather is the word used to describe the different conditions in our environment at a certain time. We can have rainy and cold weather, sunny and hot weather, or any other combination in between. You may prefer one over the others, but all types of weather are important for the environment.

Complete the following statements:

Yea, for the Sun! It helps us _____

_____

_____

It can also _____

_____

_____

Hooray for the snow! Because of it we can _____

_____

_____

But _____

_____

_____

Good for the rain! We need it because

_____

But_____

_____

The wind moves our air and helps us by

_____

_____

It can also _____

_____

My favorite weather is _____

_____

Because of it we can_____

_____

But_____

_____

I think it is scary when_____

_____

Name(s)_____

OUTDOOR PUZZLES

Nature is not just found in parks, woodlands, and mountains. It is as close as your own backyard!

I've put some of my favorite things found in nature in a word maze. See if you can find them, then you design a word maze with your own list of favorites.

Circle these words.

Clouds	Fog
Rain	Wind
Butterflies	Snow
Pines	Moon
Birds	Beach

My Puzzle

S	P	I	N	E	S	B
S	H	E	L	L	S	U
F	N	O	P	X	E	T
L	B	E	A	C	H	T
O	I	C	D	E	F	E
W	R	A	I	N	G	R
E	D	M	F	N	H	F
R	S	N	O	W	I	L
S	O	P	G	I	J	I
Q	M	O	O	N	K	E
C	L	O	U	D	S	S

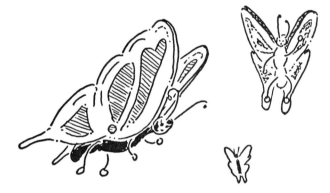

Your Puzzle

Your List

Name(s) _____

LEARN-A-LEAF

Detecting the differences in leaves is one of the ways we can identify trees. How can you learn more about leaves? For one thing, look at them very carefully.

To Do:

Carefully pick a leaf from your neighborhood, a park, or school yard. Research to find out what kind of tree it came from. Write a description of your leaf in the space below. Provide as much information as you can using your sense of sight and touch. Appreciate its beauty!

Sharp Eyes
Rough? Color? Bumpy? Ridges? Spots? Shape? Shiny? Smooth? Round?

(cut here)

_____'s Leaf
(your name)

_____
_____
_____
_____
_____
_____
_____
_____
_____
_____
_____
_____

Name(s)_____

I TOOK A WALK

I took a walk the other day,
Through the woods and to a stream.
The only sound that I could hear
Was water, swift and clear.

I passed on to a clearing
With canopy above.
I shared my space with wildlife,
All animals I love.

The squirrels chattered happily,
And jumped from tree to tree.
A timid fawn with eyes so large,
Peeked out and looked at me.

A blue jay landed on a branch,
Chirped, "Who's afraid of you?"
He scolded as I laughed at him,
Then far away he flew.

I slowly took a sweet, deep breath.
(Hemlock and pine were there.)
No smog, no soot, no fumes, or smoke!
Just wonderful clean air.

Now find yourself a special place,
Sit back and look around.
Take notes, then write about
The good things that you have found!

A Special Place

_____
_____
_____
_____
_____
_____
_____
_____
_____

Name(s) _____

CRITTER POEMS

Have you ever written haiku or cinquains? These special types of poems are fun, but be careful. You must follow the formula. Write two poems of your own using each type of formula. Read through the examples provided before you begin.

Haiku

Line 1 - 5 syllables
Line 2 - 7 syllables
Line 3 - 5 syllables

Fish

Fish are quite swishy
In the oceans and
   the pond.
I like to watch
   them.

Cinquain

Line 1 - One word title
Line 2 - Two words describing the title
Line 3 - Three words describing an action
Line 4 - Four words expressing a feeling
Line 5 - A different word for the title

Turtle
Green, quiet
Moves very slowly
Must feel safe there
Tortoise

You do these.

More: Now draw your favorite "critter" shape on the back of this page. Write your own poetry or prose on it.

Name(s)_____

ROCKY THE RACCOON

Did you know that raccoons are nocturnal and omnivorous? That means they sleep during the day and eat all kinds of food, both plants and animals. Raccoons are medium-sized mammals that look as if they are wearing Halloween masks. That reminds me of a story. I'll tell the beginning of it, and you can finish it.

Hey! Are you following me?

One October day I was walking to my friend's house. All of a sudden, I saw a raccoon come out of a hollow tree. He tiptoed quietly and quickly looked all around to be sure that no one saw him. He did not see me, so I decided to follow him. I wondered what he was up to. What an adventure we had! _____

_____

_____

_____

_____

_____

_____

_____

_____

_____

_____

_____

_____

Finish your story on the back of this page.

_____

_____

Name(s) _____

A NEIGHBOR TO NATURE

"In wilderness is the preservation of the World."

– Henry David Thoreau

Henry David Thoreau learned to be a good neighbor to nature while growing up in Concord, Massachusetts, during the early 1800s. He quickly found that in nature he could escape from the routines of daily life. Later, he discovered that most people did not take the time to appreciate the wonder in ordinary things.

As a child, Henry liked exploring nature better than playing games with the other children. In fact, they called him "Judge" because he seemed so serious. The young boy spent much time alone in the woods and meadows, hunting for Indian arrowheads or skating on the frozen pond during the winter. He also liked to whittle and carved many small animals for children.

After graduation from Harvard University, Henry became a teacher.

He once taught ninety children in one class, but was forced to leave the school after refusing to flog his pupils when they misbehaved.

Henry Thoreau made his living in a variety of ways, but it was observing and writing about nature that made him truly happy. At the age of twenty-seven he went to Walden Pond to live alone in a small cabin that he built. He wanted to live a simple life and to write about his experiences. Many visitors came to learn from him. He called them pilgrims.

Thoreau wrote a book about his life at the pond and called it *Walden.* Today we still read his work and receive pleasure from his description of nature. His words have helped to make the world a more beautiful and peaceful place in which to live.

More: Select an ordinary living thing and observe it. Discover something about it that you've never noticed before. Use all of your senses (sight, sound, smell, touch, and taste). Use the back of the page if you need more room.

My object is _____

DRAW HERE

WRITE HERE

_____

_____

_____

_____

Name(s)_____

JOHN MUIR: A PROFILE

GREEN TEAM ASSIGNMENT

Captain _____ **Date**_____

Crew _____ _____

_____ _____

Naturalist and explorer John Muir roamed the American wilderness more than one hundred years ago. Although he was born in Scotland, he grew up in Wisconsin. On one of his most famous trips, Muir walked a thousand miles from the Ohio River to the Gulf of Mexico. He then wrote about his journey.

His plans to travel farther south and explore the jungles of the Amazon River in South America were called off due to a case of malaria he had contracted. In 1868, he instead went to California, and his travels took him through the rugged Sierra Nevada mountains. Later, he helped to form the Sierra Club and became the nation's foremost conservationist.

President Theodore Roosevelt once said that the three days he spent in the mountains discussing conservation with John Muir "were the grandest days of my life."

Today, the John Muir Trail passes through three national parks, one national monument, and four wilderness areas. It is because of people like Muir that we still have vast tracts of land that remain primitive. The great beauty of our country must be preserved for this and future generations to use and enjoy.

Think and Write:

1. What do you think conservation is? _____

_____

2. Why is it important? _____

_____

3. Do we still have explorers today? _____

_____

4. Why do you think someone would walk a thousand miles in the wilderness?____

_____

5. Why is John Muir important? _____

_____

More: Read to learn more about this remarkable man and the Sierra Club.

THE PLANT DOCTOR

One night in Missouri in the early 1860s, a band of slave raiders rode up to the farm of Moses Carver. They kidnapped his only slave, Mary, and her baby son George. They did not see her second son James, who was hiding.

Although Moses and and his wife Susan Carver sent men out to search for the raiders, Mary was never seen again. Her baby George, however, was left on the side of the road and returned to the Carvers. As Moses and Susan had no children of their own, they raised the two boys in their home. After the end of the Civil War, George and his brother were set free, but they remained in the house of Moses and Susan Carver.

George was not a strong boy, and he often stuttered. He was a happy child, though, who loved animals and plants. He spent hours in his garden and soon neighbors were calling him the "plant doctor."

George grew up to become an amazing person. Learn more about him and write the rest of his story.

_____
_____
_____
_____
_____
_____
_____
_____
_____
_____
_____
_____
_____

Name(s)_____

CREEPY THINGS

Many people hate spiders! Even though they serve a purpose, they seem creepy! However, spiders can be very interesting. Here are some facts about spiders:

1. Spiders produce silk and use it to weave webs.
2. Spiders have eight legs. Insects have six legs.
3. There are about 120 different kinds of spiders.
4. Most spiders will not bite.
5. They make their webs with their back legs.
6. The web is made of protein and can be eaten by the spider.

Now, what size vest do you want? Stand still while I measure.

Most Interesting Fact: The United States Army is planning to make bullet-proof vests from spider's silk.

Maybe spiders aren't so bad, after all!

Creepy List

Snakes, Mice, Rats, Roaches, Eels, Lizards, Slugs, Moles, Alligators, Bats, Worms, Caterpillars, Octopus, Jellyfish, Toads

Pick a creature from the Creepy List (or come up with one on your own) and do some research. What interesting facts did you learn?

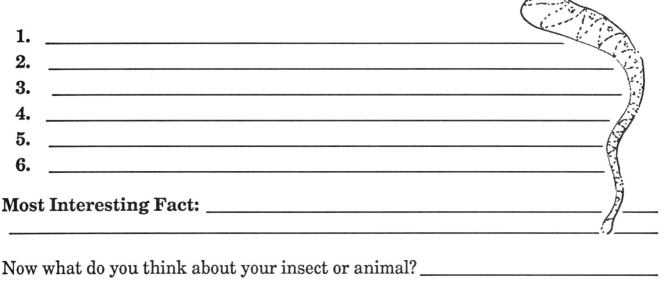

Yes sir, I think I need a 48" long.

1. _____
2. _____
3. _____
4. _____
5. _____
6. _____

Most Interesting Fact: _____

_____

Now what do you think about your insect or animal? _____

_____

Name(s) _____

BEST THINGS

"We can never have enough of Nature," wrote Thoreau. Conduct some interviews to find out what things in our environment people like best!

Let's start with me! I like sunsets and their beautiful colors the best.

Your teacher

Your parents

A school worker

Girl classmate

Boy classmate

You

Name(s)_____

EARTH WATCH: A CLOSER LOOK

The major goal of this chapter is to help students identify and understand important global and local environmental issues in an effort to encourage an active role in conservation. With direction, students can learn to recognize local environmental problems first-hand. Reading about pollution does not have the same impact on a student as does discovering it for one's self. A concrete understanding of local environmental problems will certainly lead students to a greater appreciation for worldwide conservation issues, and for teachers, a hands-on method always reaps the greatest rewards. As an old Chinese proverb says:

> I hear and I forget.
> I see and I remember.
> I do and I understand.

We also emphasize family-oriented activities in this chapter with the hope that the information learned at school can become a part of your students' daily routines.

EARTH WATCH: A CLOSER LOOK

DEFENDERS OF WILDLIFE

GREEN TEAM ASSIGNMENT

Captain _____   **Date** _____

Crew _____   _____

_____   _____

As population increases, plants and wildlife lose their natural habitats to cities and suburban areas. The World Wildlife Fund estimates that if current trends in urban development continue, almost half the species of plants and animals now in existence will be extinct by the year 2050. At stake is not only the existence of unique species which can never return, but the loss of plant substances that may be used by humans for medical and industrial advancement.

In 1992, the Endangered Species Act protected almost twelve hundred endangered plants and animals worldwide. Seven

hundred of these are in the United States. Another four thousand species are being watched carefully and may be on the threatened species list. People can do a lot to help threatened and endangered plants and animals. When some species are close to extinction, they are caught and put in safe places, like zoos, where they can survive and reproduce. This method helped to bring back the bald eagle, California condor, black-footed ferret, and the red wolf.

Find Out More:

1. Have there been recent changes in the Endangered Species Act?
2. What are some of the problems with the Endangered Species Act?
3. How does the Endangered Species Act affect industry?
4. How do you feel about the animals forced to live in captivity?
5. What do you think should be done to protect endangered species?

EYE-OPENING WORDS

What do you think about this word?

Dichlorodiphenyltrichlorethane.

whoa! This word's bigger than me.

This is the longest word found in the third edition of the *American Heritage Dictionary* and is the scientific name for the pesticide DDT. Not all words in environmental studies are quite this difficult, but some terms may still be unfamiliar to you. Below is a list of words you will want to understand. Find out the meanings of these words, then use each word in a sentence, or a paragraph, if you wish.

More: Have more fun with these words. When words are long enough, as these are, you can often make new words by rearranging the original words' letters. Choose four words or terms from the group below. How many new words can you make by rearranging their letters? We started one. Now you finish it.

Environment
_____ _____
Nine
Rot _____ _____

_____ _____

_____

Word List

Stratosphere   Extinction
Air Pollution   Overpopulation
Endangered   Biodegradable
Rain Forests   Solar Energy

_____ _____

_____ _____

_____ _____

_____ _____

_____

Name(s) _____

DIG IT UP!

Each living thing depends upon its particular environment in order to live. Soil, the loose, dirt-like material which covers most of the Earth's surface, is a part of our environment that provides food for a great number of plants, insects, and animals. Soil provides the minerals and space in which all plants can grow, and insects rely on soil to provide their nutrients. Humans, of course, plant fruits, vegetables, and grains in the soil, as well as use it for livestock grazing.

Soil erosion, however, is a serious problem throughout the world today. Because of poor farming techniques and harsh weather conditions, much soil is blown or washed away. Another threat to our soil occurs when pesticides leak into the ground from improperly disposed of waste materials.

To Do:
Bring in a small cup or jar of soil from your yard or neighborhood.

1. Compare your soil sample with others' samples. Is there a difference in the way your soil looks or feels?
2. Find out what crops are grown in your area. (Different types of soil grow different types of agricultural products.)
3. Start digging! Do some research to find out more about the soil where you live. Are there problems with the soil? If so, what is being done about them?

Choose one of the following ways to report your findings:
Write a report, make a tape (video or audio), draw several pictures, make a chart, bring in several different samples of soil and label them, or perform a soil sampling.

Name(s) _____

WOW!
BULLETIN BOARD

PURPOSE

An eye-opening bulletin board encourages students to think. Combine language arts activities with research into ecological problems, and you'll have a winner!

CONSTRUCTION

Use bright, bold letters to create the word "WOW!"
Write activity suggestions on index cards.
Use large manila envelopes for topics and process options.

USE

Write environmental topics of current interest on 3" x 5" cards. Place cards in a manila folder on the bulletin board for students to read. In the other pocket, you can offer a wide range of language arts activities for students to choose from (posters, bumper stickers, letters, book reports, poems, cartoons, rap, research papers, etc.).

Have students choose one topic card and one activity card to create a mini-research project. After the projects have been completed, place them on the bulletin board. Display your students' work by placing this board in a hallway to share with others.

WOULD I BE "LION"?

Hi, my name is Lester the Lion. Things are tough in the jungle these days. There was a time when the air and water here were clean, and there were lush trees, bushes, and flowers. Now, these things are disappearing. Some of my old buddies seem to be missing, too. Can you help me? Please write me a letter explaining what's going on out here in the jungle.

Name(s) _____

THE OCEAN

Our oceans cover more than seventy percent of the Earth's surface. Many different ecosystems and environments, ranging from mountains to jungle-like habitats, exist in the ocean. The plants and animals that thrive in these ocean habitats all depend upon each other for food. They form what is called a food chain and food web. At the bottom of the food chain are the tiny plankton. These creatures feed on plant life and then become food for small fish, which are, in turn, eaten by larger fish, and so on. At the top of the food chain are human beings.

Numerous food chains which are interconnected form a food web.

For thousands of years people have fished and enjoyed this valuable food source. What happens, though, when pollution, waste-dumping, or overfishing kills off a certain species in the oceans? Something else goes hungry, and the whole food chain becomes disturbed. Our oceans are becoming more and more polluted and overfished. People must work together to improve ocean conditions throughout the world if this valuable resource is to survive.

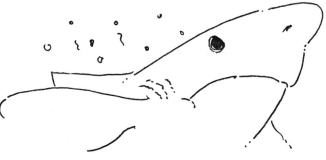

Test Your Memory

1. How much of the Earth's surface is ocean? _____

2. What is the ocean floor like? _____
_____

3. What is an extended food chain called? _____

4. What is at the bottom of the ocean's food chain? _____
At the top? _____

5. What are some of the problems in our oceans today? _____
_____
_____

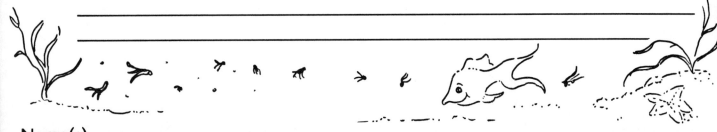

Name(s)_____

GREEN VOCABULARY

Environment
fossil fuels
recycle
wetlands extinct habitat
Pollution
smog
Biodiversity
ecosphere
species
Natural resource
toxic waste
Solar energy
wildlife refuge
Greenhouse effect
Conservation
Preservation wildlife
biodegradable

Each day of our lives, our personal vocabulary grows as we are exposed to new subjects and experiences. The field of environmental studies has created a brand new set of vocabulary words. This "green vocabulary" is especially important to learn if we are to understand current world problems.

To Do:

Select five terms from the vocabulary tree. Write them on this sheet and give a definition for each. Pick what you think is the hardest word from the group. Then do some research on that topic and write a paragraph about it on the back of this sheet.

1. _____
2. _____
3. _____
4. _____
5. _____

The hardest word is _____

Name(s) _____

43

KNOW THE FACTS

Read the statements on the Student List and check whether you think they are true or false. Then take this sheet home and read the statements on the Family List to members of your family.

Student List (True or False)

_____ 1. The car is the only source of air pollution.
_____ 2. Dumping waste products is a problem.
_____ 3. Our oceans will always be clean and safe.
_____ 4. It is not important to worry about the possible extinction of all species.
_____ 5. Solar energy is important for our future.
_____ 6. Recycling is hard and not worth it!

Family List (True or False)

_____ 1. Many cleaning products pollute the environment.
_____ 2. Leaky air conditioners harm the atmosphere.
_____ 3. Plastic foam cups are biodegradable.
_____ 4. All aerosol cans are safe for the environment now.
_____ 5. Energy efficient appliances are now being made.
_____ 6. You turn off all light switches when you are not in a room.
_____ 7. Wood-burning stoves and fireplaces pollute the air.
_____ 8. It's important to use sun screen at all hours of the day.

Together, make a family list of new things you will do to help the environment.

Name(s)_____

WHALE WATCHING

My family has been around for fifty million years. Don't you think we have the right to swim in the oceans and survive in peace?

I'm Walter, a sperm whale. Some of my friends include the white whale, the humpback whale, and the blue whale. Would you write a story about one of us? You can write your story on me!

Name(s) _____

TAKE A DEEP BREATH

Although the air in your city may look clean, air pollution is still a big problem! Our federal government regulates air pollution through the Clean Air Act, but many areas of the country are not doing as much to keep air clean as they should. What is being done to control air pollution where you live?

Facts:

The five major air pollutants are:
1. Carbon monoxide from cars and trucks
2. Ozone from factories and automobiles
3. Sulfur dioxide from industries using coal or oil
4. Nitrogen dioxide, a yellow-brownish gas from motor vehicles and factories or utility plants
5. Particle matter such as dirt, dust, or soot

My mini-poster.

Take a bike or a hike.

Stop Polluting!

To Do:

Do some research to uncover the causes of air pollution in your town and make a mini-poster to teach people how to stop its effects. Show your teacher your mini-poster, then make a larger poster to display in a special place.

Name(s)_____

SAVE OUR ENVIRONMENT

Ecology is a very important word. It is the study of all living things in their natural environments. Your environment is made up of everything you see and do.

Complete the environmental chart on the right showing important aspects of your environment. Write a descriptive word under each.

Animal List

Hawk	Prairie Dog
Seal	Porpoise
Lobster	Camel
Cat	Giraffe

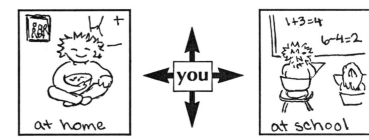

More: Choose two of the animals on the Animal List and make an environmental chart for each. Draw a habitat and write a descriptive word for each part of their environment.

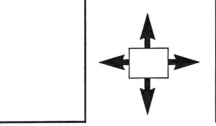

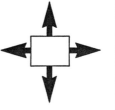

To Think About:

How would you feel if a part of your environment was taken from you? Write a paragraph discussing your response.

Name(s) _____

ON ASSIGNMENT

Littering

Cans

Trash

Drinking Cup

Paper cups

Air Pollution

Factory

Home

Your job this week is important.
First, fold this page in half. Then, make a jazzy environmental cover on the front. Write the words "Earth Notes" on the back page. Now, you are ready to go to work. Here's the assignment.

1. Keep this booklet with you at all times.
2. Whenever you see litter, make a check mark in the correct picture, or on the trash can if there is no matching picture.
3. When you see air pollution, make a check mark in the picture that shows its source, or in the cloud if there is no matching picture.
4. When you see something being done that is helpful to the environment, write about it on the back page.
5. At the end of a week, count the check marks and record the total.
6. Share all information with your class!

TOTALS

Litter _____
Cups _____
Cans _____
Paper _____
Trash _____

AIR POLLUTION

Homes _____
Factories _____
Vehicles _____
Other _____

Name(s) _____

FRIENDLY REMINDERS

Write messages on these critters to give to friends and family members. This is a great way to say thanks for helping the environment or to give a friendly reminder to do better.

Use it again, again and again!

Something Fishy!

Think Grrreen!

"Earthwatch"

Name(s) _____

A GLOBAL PERSPECTIVE

Let's look at the environment beyond our own town and country. What is happening in the world? Can you transfer these numbers into graphs?

like this

Nitrous Oxides 6%

Other 7%

Methane 12%

Carbon dioxide 54%

Chlorofluorocarbons 21%

These gases contribute to global warming.

Choosing from the information provided below, make two graphs.

1. **Wildlife Habitat Loss:**
   Vietnam 80%   Cameroon 59%
   South Africa 57%   Indonesia 49%

2. **Farmland Lost Worldwide:** Completely 14.8%   Temporarily 51.9%

3. **Threatened Seafood Supply due to Worldwide Overfishing:**
   1975-1980 - 70.1 million metric tons
   1985-1990 - 80.2 million metric tons

4. **Population of People in Asia:**
   1992 - 3,155 million   2025 - 4,976 million (projected)

5. **Percent of Land Where Quality of Soil Has Been Lowered:**

   Africa 74%   Asia 76%   Australia 55%
   Europe 72%   North America 85%   South America 76%

LINE GRAPH

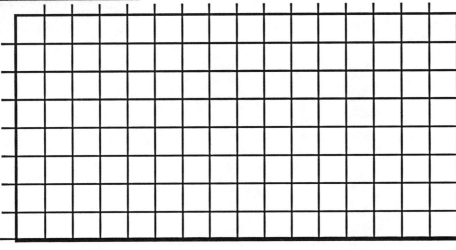

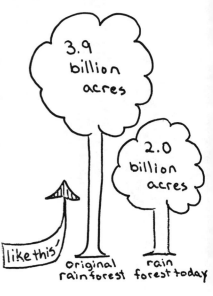

3.9 billion acres

2.0 billion acres

like this

original rainforest   rain forest today

More: On the back of this sheet make a picto-graph showing two or more of the facts you've learned. It can look like this.

Name(s)_____

WHAT'S MOST IMPORTANT

The first Earth Day was celebrated in 1970. Since then, the Earth and its environmental conditions have changed significantly.

Complicating matters further, not everyone agrees on how to solve these problems, or which ones should be solved first.

To Do:
Listed below you will see some of the problems affecting our planet today. Rewrite this list, ranking these issues in order of how important you think they are. Place what you feel is the most important issue at the top of the list and what you feel is least important at the bottom.

Waste dumping

Endangered species

Air pollution

Clean water

Overpopulation

Ozone layer depletion

Global warming

Rain forests

Fishing grounds

Natural resources depletion

Help!

Emergency

Scary

Serious

Ho Hum

1. _____
2. _____
3. _____
4. _____
5. _____
6. _____
7. _____
8. _____
9. _____
10. _____

Note: Take this sheet home and discuss it with your family. Do they agree with your choices? Why or why not?

Name(s) _____

51

SNOW BIRDS FLY SOUTH

To Play:

1. Get a partner.
2. Get two buttons.
3. Roll a die.
4. Move the marker.
5. Answer the question card.
6. Stay – if correct.
7. Go back – if wrong.
8. Follow directions on board.
9. Have fun!

Brr!

Go fast - Cold and windy - Move ahead two spaces.

Eeek!

Oh no - detour - Hunters! Go back one space

City smog - Can't see. Stay put - Lose turn.

No trees - only houses - Detour- back one.

Beautiful forest. Good day - Go ahead one space.

Bad Storms! Fly high - get lost. Go back one space.

Burning brush. Can't see. Lost! Stay put.

Polluted river! Yuck! Go back one space.

Ouch!

Hit by a golf ball - Detour.

Clear sky. Sunny day. go ahead one space.

Yea!

Almost there.

SOUTH

Aaaah! The beach!

Smooosh!

Name(s) _____

EARTH DAY CELEBRATION

Scene: *This play takes place on Earth Day in Anytown, USA.*

Characters: *Mr. and Mrs. Simmons, their two daughters Kirsten and Whitney, their son Jeremy, and his friend Vinny.*

ACT ONE

(The Simmons family is eating breakfast together in their home.)

Whitney: Do you know what day it is?

(No response)

Whitney: Doesn't **anyone** know what day it is?

Kirsten: I do, I do. I don't go to play school today, so it must be Saturday. Am I right?

Mrs. Simmons: Yes, Kirsten, you're right. But, I'm not sure that's what your sister means.

Mr. Simmons: What do you mean, Whitney?

Jeremy *(With mouthful, mumbles)*: Yea, what's the big deal?

Whitney: I can't believe this family! Don't you know that it's Earth Day?

Jeremy: Sure, my class planted a tree yesterday, and then we saw a movie about the rain forest. That was pretty neat, but the rain forest is so far away. Who cares, anyway?

Kirsten: I care, Whitney. I really care. What day did you say it is? Can I put my party dress on?

Mrs. Simmons *(Puts out her hand to calm the child)*: No, Kirsten. It's not that kind of a day. Today we celebrate the Earth and all the good things about it. And, we also try to do something to help it.

Whitney: Oh, let's! Let's do something special today.

Jeremy: You can count me out.

Kirsten: I'll be in, please let me be in, Whitney!

Mr. Simmons *(Laughing)*: I know what we can do. Today my men's club cleans up the road around the lake. You can all help.

Mrs. Simmons: That's a fine idea. I'll pack a picnic lunch.

Whitney: Oh, Daddy! I knew you would think of something great.

Kirsten: I'll go get my new sunglasses. I'll need my sunglasses.

Jeremy: You do that, kiddo! Me, I'm staying home.

Vinny *(Enters with a bang)*: Hi, all! What's for breakfast? Am I too late?

Mr. Simmons: No, Vinny. You're right on time. We're going on a road clean-up for Earth Day, and you can come along.

Vinny: Sounds great, Mr. S. Are we bringing any food?

Jeremy *(Groans loudly)*

EARTH DAY CELEBRATION

ACT TWO, SCENE ONE

(The group is walking along a lakeside road.)

Mrs. Simmons: You certainly are grouchy today, Jeremy. I'd think you would feel good about what you are doing.

Jeremy: Feel good? Feel good about picking up other people's garbage? Why would that make me feel good?

Mr. Simmons: I'm ashamed of you, son. Your attitude is all wrong. I know that you don't litter. You throw trash where it belongs, but there are a lot of careless people in the world and they need to be taught.

Jeremy: Well, this is just boring. I'd rather be playing baseball.

Kirsten: Hey, where's Vinny? I want him to help me with my bag.

Whitney: Look! Here he comes out of the woods.

Vinny *(Excitedly)*: Come quickly, everybody! Come see what I found!

(The family pushes bushes aside and follows Vinny.)

Vinny: See, there's an animal there, and it's standing guard over a big pile of trash.

Jeremy: Let's get a closer look.

Mr. Simmons: Not too close, kids. It's a beaver, and it looks as if it's protecting the lodge.

Whitney: What's a lodge?

Kirsten: What's a beaver?

Mrs. Simmons: A beaver is a large rodent.

Jeremy: You mean, like a rat?

Mrs. Simmons: Not exactly. Beavers gnaw with their front teeth like mice, rats, squirrels, and prairie dogs, but they can also swim.

Mr. Simmons *(Pointing to the beaver)*: Those little animals can cut down big trees. They then use them, along with rocks and mud, to build a dam. On top of that, they build a house, or lodge, where they live and store their food.

Jeremy: Wow! This is great! This is really awesome!

Vinny *(Saying proudly)*: Aren't you glad I found this?

Jeremy: Yea Vin, but look at all that junk. How can he live there? It looks like a trash heap around his house.

Kirsten: Poor Mr. Beaver.

Whitney: You're right. It's really full of junk.

Jeremy: How about if Vinny and I stay here while you guys finish on the road. You can stop back for us.

Mrs. Simmons: The water is cold, Jeremy. I'm afraid you'll get wet.

Jeremy: That's O.K., Mom. On Earth Day, we have to sacrifice a little to help others.

EARTH DAY CELEBRATION

ACT TWO, SCENE TWO

(The group is slowly walking back to the car, carrying large bags of trash.)

Kirsten: Tell me more about the beaver, Jeremy.

Jeremy: Well, it's like this. When we started moving the junk, we found a mother and some babies. Poor things were all crowded in smelly trash.

Vinny: Yea, it was some mess.

Jeremy: But, we got it all cleaned out, and the father beaver came back. I think he was happy. Hey Dad, you think we can come back next year and clean the road again?

(Mr. and Mrs. Simmons look at each other, smiling.)

Kirsten: Sure was a fun Earth Day!

RADON:
THE UNSEEN INTRUDER

Radon gas is invisible and odorless, but it can be deadly. Indoor radon is the second leading cause of lung cancer deaths in the United States. Radon gas is released by radium, which is found in the Earth's crust. The Environmental Protection Agency (EPA) estimates that four to six million homes have high radon levels. It is a potential problem for every state in our country!

Radon moves up through the soil under a building and enters it through cracks, pipes, drains, or other openings in the structure. It can also be carried into a home by water. Apartment houses can be affected by radon, too.

Inexpensive tests can be performed to detect radon levels. If your home has a high level of radon, it can easily be reduced.

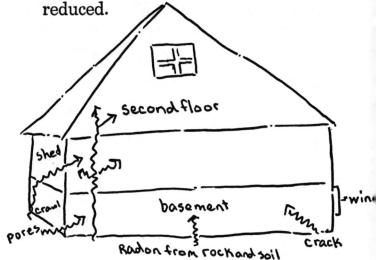

Remember:

1. Radon gas is _____ .
2. Radon can _____ .
3. Radon comes from _____ .
4. Radon enters a home by _____ .
5. Radon tests _____ .

Share this information with your family.

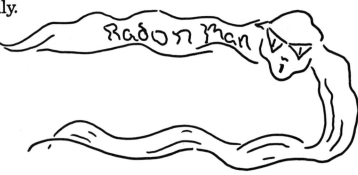

More: Contact your local American Lung Association for more information on radon gas in your area.

Name(s) _____

3

A CRY FOR HELP: ENDANGERED SPECIES

The material in this chapter explores the serious issue of endangered species. Thousands of species, both plants and animals, are disappearing at an alarming rate. The Earth is crying out for help. Part of what we hope to accomplish with this chapter is to prepare students to become future conservationists. By alerting students to a few problem areas, we hope to broaden their perspective and increase their understanding of global environmental issues. While the details are grim, we do not want to present a totally gloomy outlook. Optimism, and the knowledge that we have the ability to change the future of the planet, should be stressed in each exercise.

A CRY FOR HELP: ENDANGERED SPECIES

ON THE TRAIL OF THE DINOSAUR

Hi! My name is Theo. I'm a Tyrannosaurus. Will you please write a short story about my life?

Hundreds of dinosaur species roamed the Earth over 230 million years ago, but now they are all extinct. We know about these prehistoric creatures because their shapes have been imprinted in fossilized rock, and many dinosaur bones have been recovered and reconstructed by scientists.

Did you know that one dinosaur species became extinct approximately every ten thousand years? Today, about three species of animals become extinct each day!

Name(s) _____

GOING, GOING, GONE!

The destruction of natural habitats is one of the major reasons many animals are endangered or threatened.

Animals must live in the right surroundings in order to survive.

Write one fact you have learned about extinction and natural habitats on each of the animal shapes below.

Panda

Giant Tortoise

Sperm Whale

Name(s)_____

WHERE WE STAND

Let's look at some facts about the United States and its environmental record. Categorize the information below by placing each fact on the chart in its appropriate box. Remember to place safe environmental practices in the Plus box and harmful environmental practices in the Minus box.

1. The United States is beginning to spend more money on conservation and renewable sources research.
2. The United States emits the greatest amount of greenhouse gases worldwide, including over 20% of all carbon dioxide produced by the burning of fossil fuels.
3. The United States was the first industrial nation to regulate the amount of pollution it produced.
4. People in the United States generate twice the amount of garbage per person as do people in western Europe or Japan.
5. The United States is the leading consumer of energy per capita in the world.
6. Recycling is among the fastest growing industries in the United States. Forty-three percent of all steel produced in the Unites States is recycled.
7. The United States has lost 90% of its ancient forests and more than 221 million acres of wetlands in the lower forty-eight states.
8. The United States pioneered the concepts of wilderness preserves and national parks.

	Energy	Waste	Habitats	Air
Minus				
Plus				

More: Choose one of these statements and do some research to learn more about it. Write a report summarizing your findings.

Name(s) _____

MOTHER EARTH'S WORD

I may just be a salmon to you, but I'm King of the Hill at home.

TEACHER TIDBIT pg.153

Environmental <u>battles</u> are fought throughout the world, although not everyone agrees on how much should be done to protect endangered <u>wildlife</u> species. Many governments throughout the world, big corporations, and special interest groups see the Endangered Species Act as a hindrance rather than a necessity. They worry more about its economic impact than the global <u>protection</u> of wildlife; inconvenience and the loss of revenue are often put ahead of saving a <u>species</u>.

Can we put a price on the Pacific <u>salmon</u>, gray <u>wolf</u>, sandhill <u>crane</u>, <u>wood stork</u>, and the <u>loggerhead turtle</u>? The future of these creatures, and of all wildlife, is important to the survival of our planet as a whole. We must work to find a balance between economic development and the survival of the natural world.

To Do: The underlined words in the information above are hidden in this maze. As you find each word, circle it. Look forward, backward, up, down, and on the diagonal. This one is tricky!

a	r	w	j	i	l	n	b	a	t	t	l	e	s
p	l	o	g	g	e	r	h	e	a	d	t	t	s
r	p	o	z	d	f	l	r	z	m	s	u	n	l
o	b	d	g	h	i	w	n	o	p	q	r	a	d
t	w	s	a	l	m	o	n	e	k	n	t	x	q
e	v	t	j	c	t	s	c	k	w	o	l	f	t
c	l	o	a	d	o	i	w	s	i	b	e	r	u
t	c	r	a	n	e	d	a	v	l	i	d	m	e
i	m	k	s	s	t	e	v	s	d	i	d	w	n
o	o	e	r	o	p	e	f	i	l	c	u	m	b
n	r	o	e	r	o	p	e	s	t	w	o	e	r

Name(s) _____

CELEBRITIES OF NATURE
BULLETIN BOARD

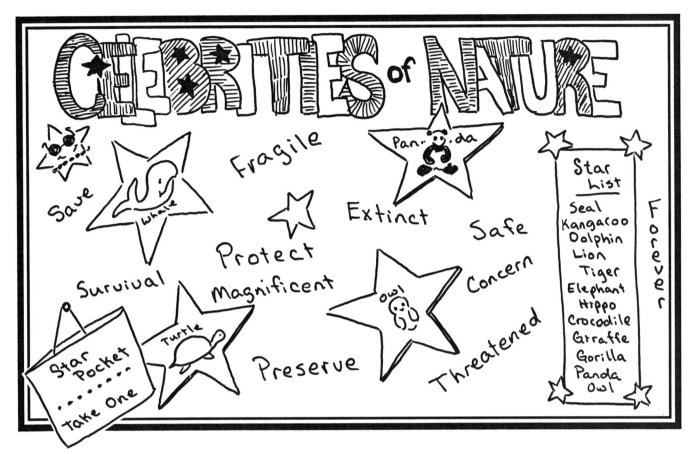

PURPOSE

Students do research and write reports to learn more about the beautiful creatures of the Earth that are in danger of extinction.

CONSTRUCTION

Cover your bulletin board with blue or green paper and brightly colored letters. Cut out large, light-colored stars, and place them in a manila envelope or folder on the bulletin board.

USE

As a class, make a list of well-known animals that are currently on the threatened or endangered species list. After the list is completed, post it on the bulletin board. Each student will select an animal from the list, research the animal's behavior and habitat, and write a short report. Final copies of student reports can be written on the backs of stars. On the fronts of the stars, have each student write the name of the animal and include its picture. Place the final reports on the bulletin board for all to read.

RAP FOR THE WORLD!

Read our rap and feel the beat. Then, write one of your own.

Extinct means gone, like here no more.
Never coming back, just out that door.

Now, that's not too good, in fact it's really bad.
The very thought just makes me mad.

Let's get to work to help one another,
It's up to us, yea, you'n me, brother!

All animals should be safe and free.
Next thing you know, extinct means ME!

Exchange your rap with another student. Read each other's rap aloud.

your rap goes here

Name(s)_____

TO SAVE THE BLUEBIRD

Bluebirds are found throughout North America. These migratory birds are easy to identify by their brilliant blue plumage. They prefer cultivated land and like to rest in the hollows and holes of trees. They also enjoy resting in artificial bluebird boxes. Unfortunately, there has been a drastic decline in the bluebird population during the past fifty years.

There are many reasons for the decline in numbers of these beautiful birds. In recent years, many farmers have changed their agricultural practices and are using toxic pesticides. The birds now avoid their former habitats of farmyards, feed lots, and tobacco barn smokestacks. Their other habitats are also diminishing as cities and suburbs are being built in formerly rural areas. Bluebirds tend to shy away from heavily populated areas.

In addition to threats by humans, bluebirds must contend with many harmful natural elements. Severe weather can be especially treacherous for them. In the wild, bluebirds must watch for predators such as raccoons, snakes, opossums, chipmunks, cats, mice, and squirrels. Starlings and house sparrows are also natural predators of bluebirds. Starlings reach into a bluebird's nest and peck at the eggs, and sparrows sometimes destroy the eggs. Many new predators have emerged in recent years as missing links in the food web cause some animals to change their hunting patterns.

The bluebird population is now on the rise due to the emergence of nonthreatening green areas such as golf courses, parks, lawns, cemeteries, farmlands, orchards, and lightly wooded areas. Bluebird boxes are catching on, and environmentalists all over the United States are reaching out to help.

FILL IN THE CHART ▼

Bluebirds are declining due to:	
Predators of the bluebird are:	
Bluebirds are helped by:	

To Do: Make a nesting box. Use a recycled plastic jug with holes cut in the bottom for drainage. Cut an opening on the side and face it south or southeast. The bluebird needs your help!

Name(s) _____

CARE FOR ME

Many animals need our help in order to survive! Write the name of each animal on the line below its picture, then match each animal to its cry for help by drawing a line from the animal to the proper word balloon.

Too many loggers are after my home.

My coat looks better on me than you!

This nice zoo gives me lots of bamboo to eat.

My eggs are not safe. The beach is too busy!

_____   _____

_____   _____

Write what you think each animal is saying in the blank word balloons.

_____   _____

To Think About: In your own words, write a paragraph explaining why you feel these animals are in trouble.

Name(s)_____

CONSERVATION WORD POWER

Here are some words we need to understand if we are to become informed conservationists. Write a definition for each of the following words:

Conservation _____

_____

Predator _____

_____

Endangered _____

_____

Threatened_____

_____

Preserve _____

_____

Fragile _____

_____

Can you think of any more conservation words?
Make a list of other conservation words you know.

_____   _____

_____   _____

_____   _____

_____   _____

_____   _____

Oooh! How did you think of that word? Quick, think of another one!

Write a sentence using each of the following words:

1. Habitat _____

_____

2. Extinction _____

_____

3. Survive _____

_____

4. Toxic _____

_____

Name(s) _____

UPDATE: MYTHS OR FACTS

TEACHER TIDBIT pg.154

Although most people want to help save the environment, not everyone agrees on how to go about doing it. In order to make the right decisions about helping our world, we need to examine all available information. We must be able to decide what information is based in fact (scientific proof) and what is based in myth (a person's opinion).

First read the following statements. Then write in "M" for myth or "F" for fact after each one. Next, compare your answers with those of a classmate. Finally, take this page home, and find out how much your family knows. Share the facts!

		You	Family
1.	Poorly managed grazing lands have damaged fragile ecosystems in some areas.	___	___
2.	Destroying South American rain forests cannot hurt the rest of the world.	___	___
3.	Global carbon dioxide levels are rising, and average temperatures are increasing.	___	___
4.	Volcanoes put less pollution in the atmosphere than vehicle emissions and industrial waste.	___	___
5.	If we burn less fossil fuels we will cause less acid rain and smog.	___	___
6.	Holes in the ozone layer at the North and South Poles are seasonal.	___	___
7.	Overexposure to bright sunlight can be harmful.	___	___
8.	Most of our household cleaners will biodegrade in thirty days.	___	___
9.	"Green cleaners" do not biodegrade at a faster rate than other cleaners.	___	___
10.	This country will never run out of space for landfills.	___	___

More: On the back of this sheet, write a major concern for the environment that you and your family have. Discuss how you think this issue could be resolved.

Name(s)_____

TEARS FOR TINY

Early one morning Alex and his dad were walking along a
deserted beach in Cape Cod. It was a warm, sunny day, and Alex
stopped along the way to pick up shells. He now had one for almost
everyone in his class back in Ohio. The two rounded a point and saw a
crowd of people. "Oh," said Alex, "what's going on over there?"
"Beats me," said his dad. "Let's go see."
The little boy and his father moved through the group. When they finally got to the
middle of the circle, they were surprised to see a huge gray whale lying on the sand.
Alex looked at the sad faces around him. "Is he dead?" Alex asked.
He pulled at the sleeve of the man standing next to him. "Mister, is he dead?"
"Yes, son," the man replied. "It must have washed up on the beach during the night."
Alex quickly turned and pushed his way through the group. He ran down the beach,
ignoring his father's calls. Faster and faster he ran.
"Hey, wait up, Alex! Wait for me!"
The boy jumped over some large rocks and continued until he was out of sight of the
beached whale. He and his dad then began to walk slowly and talk about the things
that could have happened to the dead whale. Things like disease, a serious injury, or
old age.
"How old do you think they get to be, Dad?"asked Alex.
"Well, I think about twenty years for a small whale and about seventy years for a
larger whale species is a good age."
"It didn't look that old to me," Alex said sadly.
"Wow, look at that. Something else is on the beach up ahead."
 The two ran quickly over the sand and came to a little whale lying at the
 edge of the water.
  "Oh, Dad, it's breathing. It's looking right at me. Please, we
  have to help it!"
  "Okay, stay calm. Let's think about what we can do. That must
  have been the mother whale back there."
   Alex reached down and splashed some water over the
   little whale. "It's okay, Tiny. I have a plan."

Use the back of this page to write the rest of the story.

Name(s) _____

DEFORESTATION: THE DESTRUCTION OF A RAIN FOREST

GREEN TEAM ASSIGNMENT

Captain _____   **Date**_____

Crew   _____   _____

    _____   _____

All plants, animals, and their habitats are interrelated. The species and habitats that are linked within a specific area are called ecosystems. When one part of an ecosystem disappears, an entire species can be lost forever. Many ecosystems, including the tropical rain forests, are being destroyed.

The tropical forests that still exist in South America, Africa, and Asia serve an essential purpose for the entire world. Their lush vegetation absorbs carbon dioxide (CO_2) from the Earth's atmosphere. Giant tropical rain forests once covered some five billion acres on Earth. Now, about half of the original forests have been chopped down and burned. Recently, areas as large as the state of Kansas have been destroyed in one year. This is called deforestation. As these forests are burned, the CO_2 in the plants is released into the Earth's atmosphere. Because CO_2 retains heat in the atmosphere, an excess of CO_2 could cause world temperatures to rise. This phenomenon is known as the greenhouse effect.

About half of all the Earth's plant and animal life once lived in the rain forests. Many of these exotic plants provide important materials used by drug companies in the manufacturing of life-saving medical products. Scientists are still analyzing the rain forests' plants in order to determine their usefulness to the world.

What can you do to help save tropical rain forests from destruction?

1. Ask parents and friends not to buy tropical wood products.
2. Spread the word! Don't buy animals or plants taken illegally from the rain forest.
3. Make a list of your team concerns on the back of this page. Find out what is being done by government agencies or other associations dedicated to saving the world's rain forests.

Name(s)_____

ECO-TRIP

NAME _____ DATE _____

TRIP DESTINATION _____

REMEMBER TO BRING _____

_____

SPECIAL INSTRUCTIONS_____

_____

1. What types of ecosystems do you see as you travel? _____

_____

2. What do you see that is good for the environment?_____

_____

3. What do you see that is bad for the environment?_____

_____

4. What measures have been taken to protect the area? _____

_____

5. List any litter or damage to the environment that you noticed._____

_____

6. Did you see an environmental problem today? Describe it._____

_____

7. What was the best part of your day?_____

_____

Check off any of these environmental warning signs you see throughout the course of the day.

_____ factory smoke   _____ dead animals or fish
_____ litter on ground   _____ posted regulations or warnings
_____ graffiti   ignored
_____ dirty water   _____ vehicle exhaust

THE MANATEE NEEDS HELP

GREEN TEAM ASSIGNMENT

Captain _____   Date _____

Crew _____   _____

_____   _____

The West Indian manatee is a large, gray-brown mammal that lives in tropical waters. It has a seal-like body which tapers to a tail that is flat and shaped like a paddle. The sea cow, as it is also called, can reach a length of over thirteen feet and weigh more than three thousand pounds. The manatee is not known for its appealing looks; its head and face are wrinkled, and its snout has stiff whiskers.

The legend of the mermaid is thought to have originated from sightings of these aquatic creatures. Although the manatee does not have long, golden tresses, its somewhat human-like form with tail flukes that resemble legs and forearms might lead a lonesome, near-sighted sailor to dream.

The placid manatee spends most of the day feeding and resting. Although the manatee swims under water, it must surface to breathe every five minutes or so. Because of this, the manatee is in constant danger of being killed or maimed by speeding boaters as it nears the water's surface. Some manatees are being tagged in order to study their habits and better protect them from harm. The manatee is also protected under the Endangered Species Act. "Slow Speed," "Caution," and "No Entry Zone" signs are often posted to warn boaters in populated areas. A popular slogan used to caution boaters is: "The manatee, miss her now, or forever."

How Well Did You Read?

1. Where are manatees found? _____
2. What is another name for the manatee? _____
3. How do manatees spend their time? _____
4. Use eight words to describe the manatee. _____
   _____
5. What is the biggest threat to the manatee? _____
6. Can you think of other problems manatees may encounter? _____
   _____
7. On the back of this page, write what you think the slogan "The manatee, miss her now, or forever" means.

Name(s) _____

We Recycle!

REDUCE, REUSE, AND RECYCLE: CONSERVATION IN PRACTICE

As with many habits, conservation begins at home. The conservation of our natural resources must be a family affair, as well as a personal commitment, if it is to become a permanent part of one's lifestyle. The activities and exercises presented in this chapter are intended as a means of introducing young people to daily conservation practices that can be implemented outside the classroom such as reducing waste, saving energy, and protecting the local environment. Helping students at an early age understand that conservation is a simple and effective way of protecting their world will hopefully lead them to become environmentally active adults.

REDUCE, REUSE, AND RECYCLE: CONSERVATION IN PRACTICE

THE CHASING ARROWS

GREEN TEAM ASSIGNMENT

Captain _____   **Date** _____

Crew _____   _____

_____   _____

The mobius loop, the three arrows chasing each other in a circle, has become the international symbol for recycling. The first arrow represents a

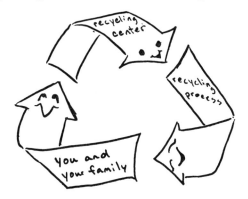

recycling center in your home or school where the products you intend to recycle are separated. All you need for this task are boxes or cans labeled for glass, metal, plastic, and paper. Glass should be separated by color (brown, green, and clear). Once separated, these items are picked up by a waste management company or transported to a local recycling center. The next arrow in the circle represents the

actual recycling process. For example, here's how newspaper is recycled.

1. Your old papers are unloaded at a paper mill.
2. They travel on conveyer belts through water.
3. The wet paper is torn apart by cutting wheels or blades.
4. The ink is removed by adding chemicals.
5. The soggy paper, called slurry, is rinsed and checked for staples and paper clips.
6. As it moves along the belt, the paper is dried and flattened by big rollers.
7. The recycled paper is wound into huge rolls and cut into sheets.

The third arrow represents you and your family closing the loop. This involves your buying recycled products. It is important to look for the mobius loop on products when you go to the grocery store.

Team Research: Complete one of the following exercises and write a report to present to the class.

1. Find out more about your local waste management company.
2. Learn more about the recycling center nearest you.
3. Find out how another material besides paper is recycled.
4. You plan a topic. Be sure to have your teacher approve it first.

TEAM TUNES

GREEN TEAM ASSIGNMENT

Captain _____   **Date** _____

Crew   _____   _____

                   _____   _____

All teams need to be cheered on! Sing our song to the tune of "I've Been Working on the Railroad." Sing it again, louder!

Now, put your heads together, and write your own team song. Pick a favorite tune, and write some new words for it. Practice your team tune, then sing it to the class.

I am working with the Green Team,
All the live long day.
I am working with the Green Team
Just to find a better way.

We are learning conservation,
Saving energy,
Working hard to keep our planet
Green for you and me.

GREEN RAP

The beat goes on, and the "green" movement grows!

Read our rap song. We hope you like it! Now, think about what it means to be a good conservationist, and write some conservation-related rhyming words in the box. Put your words together, and write your own "green" rap song. Share it with your friends.

Rube

My name is Rube.
I've been around.
I leave my trash
All over town.

I drop my cans,
My papers fall,
They fly away,
I leave them all.

A little kid
Then came along.
He picked up stuff,
And sang a song.

He talked about
The Earth so green.
He made me feel
Real bad and mean.

He told me stuff
Like "Clean it now,
Recycle things."
He showed me how.

Now I too sing
The Green Team Song.
Let's all pitch in,
Let's move it along!

— I'm Rube. I'm starting to learn the Green Team Rap. See, I picked up my trash! I guess I'll take a bath next. Yikes!

Name(s) _____

DID YOU KNOW?
A RECYCLING CHECKLIST

The average American produces more than 1,000 pounds of trash per year; we have become a "throw-away society." Many products we throw away can be reused or recycled. Here are some tips to help you recycle items found around your home. How many of these did you know already? Check the appropriate box as you read.

	YES	NO
ALUMINUM Rinse cans and crush to save space. Test with a magnet to be sure the can is aluminum, not tin. If it is aluminum, the magnet will not stick.	☐	☐
TIN The insides of tin cans are yellowish in color. Rinse, crush, and check with a magnet to make sure all material is tin. Tin will stick to a magnet.	☐	☐
GLASS Rinse, remove lids, and sort colors (clear, green, brown). Labels can be left on. Do not include light bulbs or window glass.	☐	☐
PAPER Tie, or put in paper bags. Sort paper according to type: newspapers, office, cardboard, etc.	☐	☐
MOTOR OIL Do not mix with other oils. Put in a leak-proof container, and bring to a designated recycling center.	☐	☐
PLASTICS Sort according to type: soft drink bottles, milk jugs, etc. Rinse and flatten.	☐	☐

Double check! Find out what is recycled in your town. Know how it is collected and where it goes.

What have you learned? Write one new, important fact that you learned from reading this page. Be sure to share your information with others!

Name(s)_____

RECYCLING FRIDGE MINDERS

You know that recycling helps to conserve natural resources. Did you also know that it reduces air pollution, saves energy, and provides employment? Recycling is important to everyone!

To Do: Make Fridge Minders.
Reread the recycling information from the previous assignment. Find out which of these materials are recycled where you live, and copy some important recycling facts and recycling center locations onto the shapes below. Cut out the shapes. You may also want to color them. Then, place a small loop of tape on the back of each of the drawings, and place them on your refrigerator at home. Now, no one will forget what and where to recycle!

I'm the Fridginator! I make sure everyone remembers the fridge minders!

THE NEWSPAPER

Soda Pop

Name(s) _____

BE A ONE TON FAMILY!

FACT

One ton of recycled post consumer waste paper saves at least seventeen trees from being cut down.

What is post consumer waste paper? It is what is commonly called garbage made up of newspapers, writing paper, paper bags, etc. When not recycled, this paper ends up in your local dump.

Another type of waste is called manufactured waste. Manufactured waste comes from paper scraps left after other products are manufactured. Much of the paper you see that is marked "100% recycled paper" is made from these materials.

FACT

One ton of recycled post consumer waste paper saves enough energy to run your home for six months.

Please, please recycle!

To Do: Write a slogan on one of the Fridge Minders. Cut it out, and take it home to remind your family to save all waste paper. Also, fill in the following chart for one week. Weigh, or count, the daily collection. What's your weekly total?

FAMILY WEIGH-IN CHART

MONDAY	
TUESDAY	
WEDNESDAY	
THURSDAY	
FRIDAY	
SATURDAY	
SUNDAY	

WEEKLY TOTAL:

Name(s) _____

HOW LONG?

While some products made from natural substances will decompose within a few years, many artificial products take thousands of years to break down. How long do you think the following objects will remain in our environment? Draw a line from the object to the years.

1.	Cigarette butts	a.	Up to 2 years
2.	Aluminum tabs/cans	b.	20 to 30 years
3.	Plastic 6-pack holder	c.	1,000,000 years
4.	Orange and banana peels	d.	5 years
5.	Plastic film container	e.	50 years
6.	Plastic bags	f.	10 to 20 years
7.	Glass bottles	g.	1 to 5 years
8.	Plastic-coated paper	h.	30 to 40 years
9.	Plastic bottle	i.	1 to 5 years
10.	Nylon fabric	j.	80 to 100 years
11.	Leather	k.	Up to 50 years
12.	Wool socks	l.	100 years
13.	Tin cans	m.	Indefinitely

Don't peek in my Banana Peel!

Answers: 1. g, 2. j, 3. l, 4. a, 5. b, 6. f, 7. c, 8. d, 9. m, 10. h, 11. k, 12. i, 13. e

How did you do? _____ Great _____ So-So _____ Need Improvement

What surprised you the most? _____

_____

_____

_____

_____

Take this home, and give the quiz to your family. How can you change your lifestyle to prevent excess trash from being thrown into a landfill?

Name(s) _____

RECYCLED WORDS

Recycling is one of the easiest ways for you to practice conservation. Many people, though, have not been taught which items can be recycled and which can be thrown away. Someone who didn't know any better threw many recyclable items into this garbage can. Dig in, and take them out by locating the items in the word maze and circling them. Then, write each word in the recycle box.

Words to locate:

Plastic bottle	Newspaper	Wire hanger
Glass bottle	Tin can	Milk jug
Paper bag	Cardboard	Detergent jug
Aluminum can	Tire	

Recycle Box

A	R	E	P	A	P	S	W	E	N	X	T	I
M	Q	S	Z	A	L	T	D	D	I	S	I	Q
A	D	I	B	H	A	G	J	M	Y	O	R	S
C	G	L	A	S	S	B	O	T	T	L	E	U
Z	P	O	N	L	T	C	J	I	H	Y	F	A
G	O	H	F	K	I	M	E	N	O	T	C	U
D	C	Q	O	P	C	D	A	C	M	D	S	J
P	A	P	E	R	B	A	G	A	I	E	R	C
A	R	E	A	N	O	B	O	N	L	F	O	H
N	D	O	B	S	T	G	Q	L	K	U	R	K
Q	B	R	Z	A	T	L	V	O	J	U	A	D
C	O	H	C	W	L	I	S	M	U	F	T	L
W	A	W	I	R	E	H	A	N	G	E	R	N
H	R	G	N	P	V	J	M	R	O	K	U	B
O	D	E	T	E	R	G	E	N	T	J	U	G
N	A	C	M	U	N	I	M	U	L	A	L	E
D	I	B	C	S	E	W	Y	L	L	V	N	D

Name(s)_____

VOICE OF THE CONSUMER

Do you wonder what steps other people are taking to reduce consumption, recycle, and avoid waste? Here's how you can find out. Be a Green Team Reporter!

Interview three to five people you do not know very well. Use the following suggestions to help your interview go smoothly:

1. Speak slowly. Introduce yourself at the beginning of the interview.
2. Ask first if you may have a few moments of your subject's time.
3. Explain your purpose. Tell your subject that you and other class members are involved in a project to learn about your neighborhood's recycling habits.
4. Use one copy of the interview page provided for each person interviewed. Read the page a few times before you begin the interview.
5. Be sure to thank each person at the end of your interview.

More: After you have finished your interviews, meet with your Green Team. Put all of your interviews together and compile a report to present to your class.

Cut here and give to person interviewed.

CONSUMER FACTS

Did you know that...

- Recycling one glass jar will save enough energy to light a 100-watt bulb for four hours.
- On average, seven trees per year are cut down to make paper and wood products for each person in the United States.
- It takes over 75,000 trees to print each Sunday edition of the *New York Times*.
- Every year Americans throw away enough steel to build a big city.
- It takes twenty trees to keep one baby in disposable diapers for two years.

HELP REDUCE WASTE BEFORE IT'S CREATED. BE A CONSCIENTIOUS CONSUMER. THE GREEN TEAM NEEDS YOU!

Name(s) _____

CONSUMER INTERVIEW

1. May I please ask your name? _____

2. The average American produces more than one thousand pounds of trash each year. Our landfills are overflowing, our natural resources will some day run out, and our toxic wastes are polluting the Earth and its atmosphere. Does this concern you? _____
    _____

3. Do you think you are a conscientious consumer? _____

4. Do you recycle:_____
    (Please circle)

    Glass   Plastics   Tin   Paper
    Scrap Metal   Aluminum   Motor oil

5. Do you have a compost heap to save organic materials for fertilizer?
    _____

6. If you have a choice, do you buy the item packaged in the most recyclable way?_____

7. Do you take your own bag or ask for paper bags instead of plastic at the grocery store? _____

8. Do you use paper plates instead of plastic ones at your picnics? ____
    _____

9. Do you look for the recycling symbol on items you buy?_____

10. Do you turn off the tap water when brushing your teeth?_____

11. Do you buy disposable goods, such as razors, batteries, pens, paper napkins, or paper towels?_____

12. What do you do that you consider a good consumer practice?_____
    _____
    _____

Name(s) _____

TO THE DUMP

Some people find recycling easy; others find it a tough job. All it takes to recycle is knowing where to dispose of things...and doing it.

Look at the pictures labeled "A" through "D." Each picture represents a different place to throw away your trash. Read the list of items to be thrown away, and decide upon the proper location for each waste item. Write the corresponding letter next to each item.

1. Plastic bread wrapper
2. Potato peels
3. Your old jeans
4. Used paper plates
5. Milk jug
6. Chicken bones
7. Peach pits
8. Peanut shells
9. Used paper towels
10. Detergent bottle
11. Glass jelly jar
12. Soda can
13. Disposable razor
14. Old chair
15. Bread crusts
16. Ham bone
17. Ball point pen
18. Broken mirror
19. Magazines
20. Green glass bottle

More: Go over your answers with other students or members of your Green Team. Are there some items on this list that are not collected for recycling in your town? What can you do about this?

Name(s) _____

SILLY WILLY NILLY

Sometimes we learn from people who we least suspect can teach us. Keep your eyes and ears open! What does Silly Willy have to teach?

*Mr. Silly Willy Nilly
Really is his name.
However, he **did** act that way.
That's how he got his fame!*

*He went to the dump one day
To see what he could find.
He gathered up a lot of stuff.
What's really on his mind?*

*Now Willy found two fenders,
A wheel that still looked good.
To them he added old tin cans,
And then he found a hood.*

*He spent the day collecting junk.
The pile it grew and grew.
His wagon seemed from outer space,
When finally he was through.*

*I followed Silly Willy
To see where he would go.
He walked for miles, then to a gate.
(Some place I did not know.)*

*The man inside the big, high fence
Seemed happy that he came.
He greeted Mr. Nilly—
He even knew his name.*

*They took the junk from place to place,
Then packed some in a van.
They saw me standing, watching them,
Said, "Help us if you can."*

*It seems that Willy Nilly
Wasn't silly after all.
"This is conservation," he said,
Standing straight and tall.*

*He told me lots of special things
About the planet Earth.
He said that all the junk he found
Did, indeed, have worth.*

*So now we all recycle,
My friends and family too—
Thanks to Willy Nilly
Who taught us what to do.*

More: Make up another adventure with Willy Nilly in it!

Name(s) _____

FOR SUPER-DUPER RECYCLERS ONLY

Be a super recycler! Buy and use recycled materials, then recycle them once again.

For many people, recycling is a way of life. In the store, we check to see whether products have the recycling symbol on them. We can also look for the words "This product is packaged in recycled paperboard." And that's good. Super-duper recyclers take it one step further and find new uses for old things, or they make old items new again. How? How about this? A tire can be hung from a tree for a swing. The old inner tube can be used as a float for swimming.

To Do: Choose four things from the junk list and think of some creative ways to reuse them. Use your imagination!

Junk List

- paper
- old socks
- grocery bags
- plastic detergent containers
- cardboard milk cartons
- frozen juice containers
- plastic milk jugs
- large cardboard boxes

1. _____

_____

_____

2. _____

_____

_____

3. _____

_____

_____

4. _____

_____

_____

Name(s) _____

A WAY OF LIFE

See me, I'm the recycle sign!

Your grandparents didn't do it when they were your age, but recycling has become a way of life in recent years. You are probably separating your glass bottles, plastic, cardboard, cans, and newspapers to be recycled. We all are. By recycling we are helping to preserve valuable resources, extending the life of local landfills, and providing alternate energy sources. This new industry also creates new jobs.

Take recycling one step further. Look for the recycling symbol on products you and your family purchase, then recycle those items when you are through with them. You *can* make a difference in the state of the environment.

To Do: Take this sheet home. Look around your house for twenty-five items that can be recycled. Be sure to check the kitchen, bathroom, and basement. Write the name of each product in the shape below where you will eventually dispose of the item. Get some help—recycling is a family job.

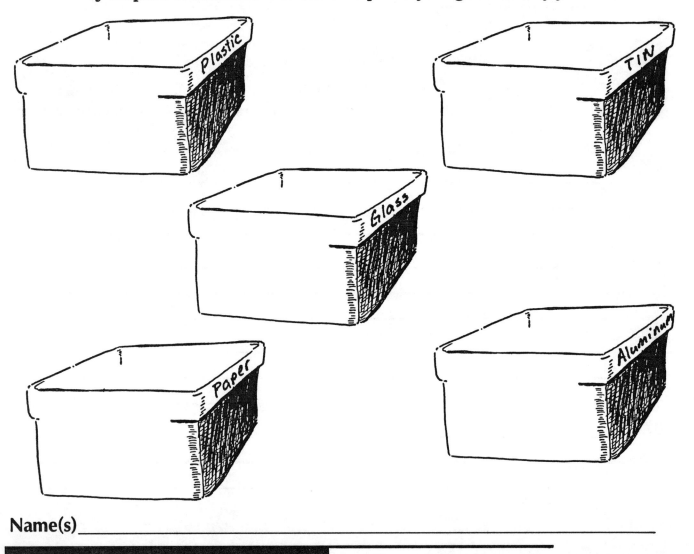

Name(s) _____

THE RECYCLING LOOP
BULLETIN BOARD

Recycle... Recycle... Recycle...

Remember!!
The recycling loop includes:
1. Separation of materials
2. Collection of materials
3. Processing materials
4. Remanufacturing into new products
5. Buying recycled products.

PURPOSE

To provide an eye-catching area where student research and reports can be attractively arranged.

CONSTRUCTION

Cover your bulletin board with bright green construction paper. Cut the three chasing arrows of the recycling symbol out of white paper. Place them on your board, and write the title inside the circle. Print the "reminder sheet" on a paper of contrasting color, and mount it on the board. Ask each student to bring in an empty soft drink can. Cut the tops off of the cans, and tack the cans to the bulletin board. Be sure to cover the cans with decorative paper to hide any sharp or rough edges!

USE

Assign students topics or themes related to recycling. As students bring in completed work, have them roll their reports and place them in cans. This provides an attractive display and easy access to the reports.

ARBOR DAY ANY DAY

Trees are an important part of our environment. Besides being beautiful and fun to climb or swing on, they serve a purpose. Trees help to keep our air clean, keep the soil healthy and stable, and provide living environments for many different kinds of animals. We can also eat the fruits and nuts from trees and make sugar from a tree's sap. Trees are also valuable as a resource and many are cut down to make paper and lumber for houses. It is important, therefore, to plant new trees to replace the ones being cut down.

Global Releaf, a project of the American Forestry Association, is dedicated to planting new trees all over the United States of America. They provided the following instructions on how to plant a tree. Try it! Hold a classroom or school fundraiser to buy the trees, then plant them and watch them grow.

HOW TO PLANT A TREE FOR A COOLER, CLEANER WORLD

1. Locate a clear, open site for your tree, with generous rooting area and good drainage.
2. Loosen and blend the soil in the entire planting area 6 to 10 inches deep. In the center, dig a hole at least as wide, but only as deep as the root ball.
3. Remove tree from burlap or container and place on solidly packed soil so that the root collar (where the tree's main stem meets the roots) is slightly above the surrounding grade.
4. Backfill the hole and lightly pack the soil into place around the tree.
5. Spread a 2- to 3-inch layer of mulch in the entire area, keeping a 6- to 8-inch distance from the tree trunk.
6. Stake the tree so that it can flex in the wind. Attach stake to the tree by using discarded rubber inner tubes. Remove them after six months.
7. Water thoroughly, but do not flood the hole. Water twice a week during dry periods.

Rubber Tubing or Hose

Flexible Stake Attached to Tree

Prepared Soil

Rootball, 18 INCHES wide

Burlap

Existing soil

Name(s)_____

MEETING THE CHALLENGE:
LEARNING TO SPEAK OUT ABOUT
ENVIRONMENTAL ISSUES

Today's young people are faced with a great many environmental dilemmas. Upon maturity, they will inherit a host of problems ranging from the depletion of natural resources and how and where to dispose of garbage to the effects of toxic substances on the atmosphere. As a teacher, it is important to first make young people aware of these problems and then to stress that they have the power to change current conditions. The exercises in this chapter teach children that they can have a voice in their community, that they can be heard. If children learn at an early age to speak up on behalf of the environment, it is likely that they will continue to take an active part in both local and national environmental issues throughout their lives.

These exercises also promote fundamental learning skills, such as research, vocabulary development, creative writing, critical thinking, and mathematics. Teamwork and cooperative learning skills are also stressed in the Green Team activities provided.

MEETING THE CHALLENGE: LEARNING TO SPEAK OUT ABOUT ENVIRONMENTAL ISSUES

GROUP GOALS

When working with a group such as your Green Team, everyone's ideas are important! A step-by-step plan is often useful to maintain order and to promote unity within the group. Through cooperation and group management, we can learn from each other. Good ideas can become great ideas when we work as a team.

Cut out the chart below, and paste it onto a piece of construction paper. Keep it in your notebook for future use. You may also find it useful when making family plans.

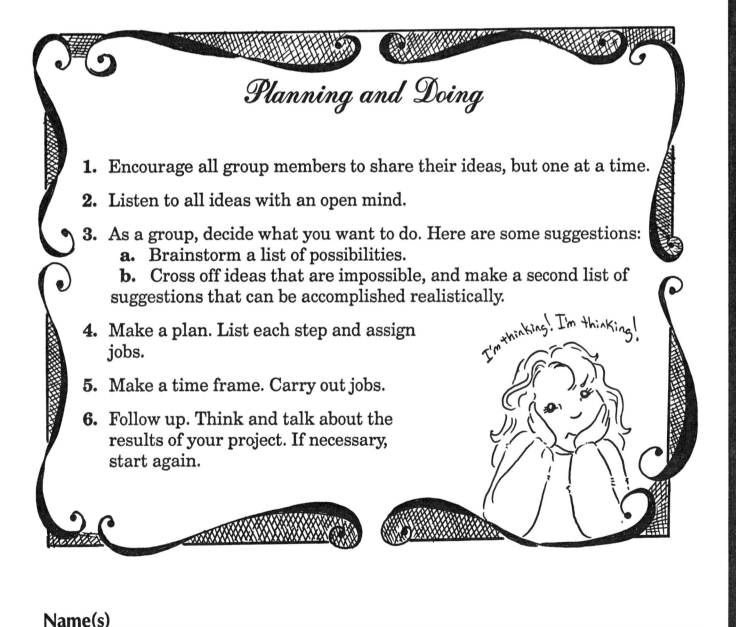

Planning and Doing

1. Encourage all group members to share their ideas, but one at a time.

2. Listen to all ideas with an open mind.

3. As a group, decide what you want to do. Here are some suggestions:
    a. Brainstorm a list of possibilities.
    b. Cross off ideas that are impossible, and make a second list of suggestions that can be accomplished realistically.

4. Make a plan. List each step and assign jobs.

5. Make a time frame. Carry out jobs.

6. Follow up. Think and talk about the results of your project. If necessary, start again.

I'm thinking! I'm thinking!

Name(s) _____

SHARE THE FACTS

TEACHER TIDBIT pg.156

Taking a stand on a particular issue is easy. Sharing what you have learned with others is the next step, but sometimes that can be hard to do.

The following exercise will help you to learn how to stand up for your beliefs, as well as how to present them politely to others.

Read each of the scenarios below, and write a paragraph describing how you would respond to each situation having just completed a unit on conservation in school.

Scene One
You and your family have gone to your grandmother's house for a cookout. You are asked to help by setting out the tableware. Your grandmother gives you plastic plates, knives, and forks to put on the picnic table. What is wrong? What can you do or say?

Scene Two
You are visiting a cousin for a week-long vacation. As you help with the dishes one evening, you notice that your aunt is running the water continuously as she rinses all of the dishes. You also discover that everyone in the family lets the water run continuously as they brush their teeth. You have been studying water conservation in school and know that water shortage is a serious problem. What do you do?

Scene Three
Your mom's friend recently had a baby girl, and they came to your home for a visit. When the baby needed changing, her mom took out disposable diapers. What can you tell her?

Name(s)_____

EARTH DAY

GREEN TEAM ASSIGNMENT

Captain _____   **Date** _____

Crew _____   _____

_____   _____

The first Earth Day celebration was held in 1970 in the United States and is the brain child of former Senator Gaylord Nelson of Wisconsin. Nelson was shocked when he noticed the rapid deterioration of our country's beautiful lakes, forests, beaches, and rivers during the 1960s. He was concerned about factories polluting the air, chemicals used by farmers on our agricultural products and soil, and people tossing litter in our lakes and streams. When a California oil leak spilled into the Pacific Ocean and killed countless birds, ducks, sea lions, and other sea creatures, Senator Nelson took action. He felt it was time for all Americans to take action.

On April 22, 1970, he gathered together interested people to give speeches, write letters, and inform the public of environmental issues. This celebration became known as Earth Day and is held every year.

On April 22, 1990, Earth Day was celebrated for the first time around the world. Since then, major summit meetings have been held in order to plan worldwide environmental programs and increase people's awareness of conservation issues.

We need to treat every day like Earth Day. How can we do this? One of the best ways to help the environment is to pass tougher laws regulating pollution. Before too long, people your age will be making these laws and helping to run the country. Show your concern now. Don't wait.

To Do: Find out what environmental issues are important in the town or state where you live. Write to your mayor or congressman to find out more. Or, best of all, write to the President of the United States. Let people know that you care about your world. Start thinking about your future today.

Name(s) _____

EARTH DAY REVISITED

Don't wait for a national Earth Day celebration. Plan your own now! Here are a few ideas to get you started. Brainstorm with your Green Team to come up with a plan for a Super Earth Day celebration, and be sure to carry it through.

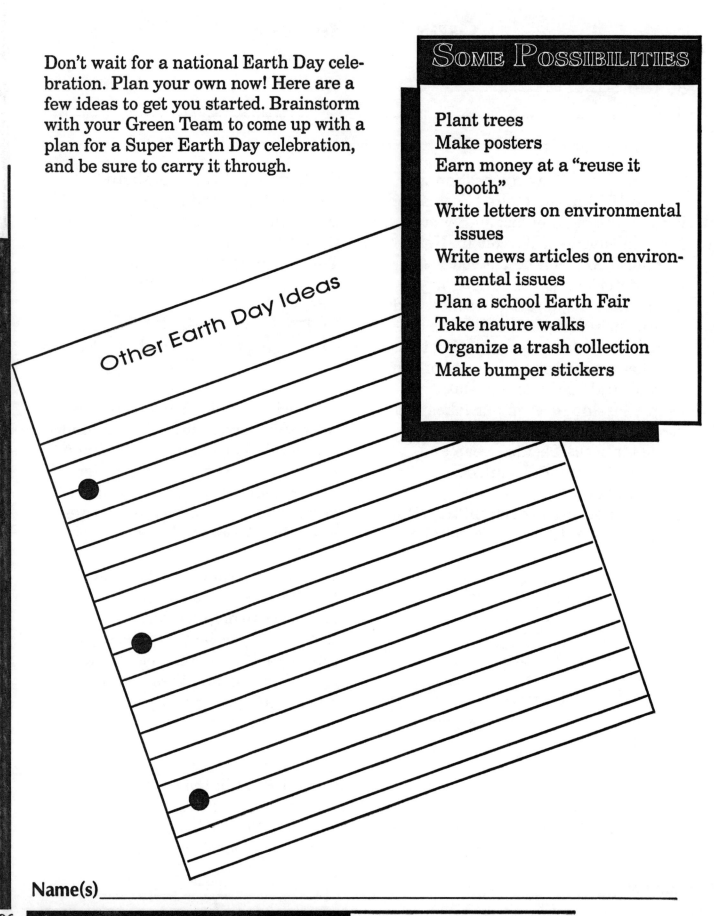

Other Earth Day Ideas

SOME POSSIBILITIES

Plant trees

Make posters

Earn money at a "reuse it booth"

Write letters on environmental issues

Write news articles on environmental issues

Plan a school Earth Fair

Take nature walks

Organize a trash collection

Make bumper stickers

Name(s)_____

THE CAN OF TUNA

GREEN TEAM ASSIGNMENT

Captain _____   **Date** _____

Crew _____   _____

_____   _____

Not too long ago, a young boy read an article about the struggle to stop the slaughter of dolphins. Dolphins are often caught in large nets set in the ocean to trap tuna fish. The dolphins that happen to fall into these traps are needlessly maimed or killed, then thrown back into the sea.

The more the boy learned, the more angry he became. He talked about the plight of the dolphins to his family, friends, classmates, and teachers. Everyone agreed that this was not right; however, they all wondered what they could do about it. How could they fight the large tuna fish corporations?

Little by little a plan emerged. The boy and other students in his class organized a campaign. They bombarded the chief executive officers (CEOs) of a major tuna canning company with postcards. Every day a few complaints were sent to the homes of the CEOs, where they were eventually read by the entire family. The children of the CEOs entered into the campaign and urged their parents to make changes in the fishing process.

It worked! Because of the concern and persistence of one young boy, the company now advertises its "dolphin-free" tuna.

To Do: Kids can and must make a difference. Is there an environmental problem in your community or state that especially concerns you? Discuss with your Green Team to come up with an environmental issue which interests you. Then make a plan to change the situation or solve the problem.

Name(s) _____

A KID'S VIEW

Today there are many warning signs indicating that our lifestyle is harming our planet. What is being done to save the natural world from danger? Organizations such as the World Wildlife Federation, the National Wildlife Federation, and the Environmental Protection Agency are just a few of the countless groups that are working hard to preserve and monitor the environment's health. You can help, too!

Brainstorm for information to complete these unfinished sentences. Use the back of this sheet if you need more space to write.

1. Many plants and animals are in danger because _____ .

2. Food chains and food webs are important because _____ .

3. Losing tropical rain forests is a threat because _____ .

4. Many types of cattle and crops can't survive without human help because _____ .

5. Public beaches are sometimes closed to swimmers because _____ .

6. The sun's rays have become more harmful to our skin because _____ .

I'm split between writing about the rain forest and the sun's rays. Get it—I'm split!! Hee! Hee!

More: Choose one topic from the list above that interests you and write to an organization of your choice for more information. Your teacher will provide you with names and addresses. Do some research, and write a report discussing the situation you researched and the information you gained.

Name(s)_____

A MILLION AND ONE TIMES

Poppa Dad, those humans only left their footprints!

Read the beginning and ending of this story, then write the middle yourself.

"When my father used to take me into the woods, he always reminded me to leave nothing but my footsteps," said Mr. Anderson.

"Yea, Dad. We know. You've told us that a million times," said Melissa.

"A million and one," chimed in her little brother Toby.

"Now kids," said Mrs. Anderson. "Your father just wants you to grow up to be good conservationists."

_____

_____

_____

_____

_____

_____

_____

_____

_____

_____

_____

_____

_____

_____

_____

_____

"Well kids, I'm really proud of you. You showed us that you know all the right things to do to preserve our natural world. Guess I don't have to remind you ever again."

Name(s) _____

TRASH SPLASH
BULLETIN BOARD

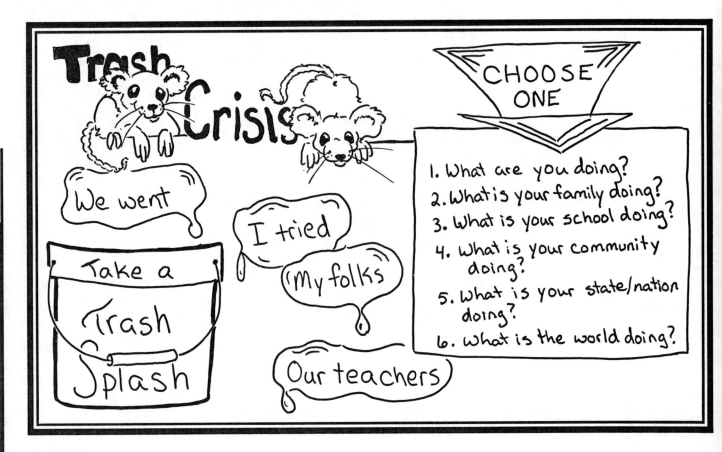

PURPOSE
Students do research and write reports about current trash dilemmas. Students should be encouraged to come up with new methods for improving the trash crisis.

CONSTRUCTION
Cover your bulletin board with old newspapers. Cut letters from black construction paper to spell the word "Trash." List the research topic options on chart paper. Cut "splashes" out of brightly colored paper on which to mount reports.

USE
Discuss the mounting trash problem in landfills and in our oceans. Also discuss alternate ways to dispose of waste, such as the trash-to-steam method and recycling. Ask students what they can do individually to help solve the trash problem.

Have students choose topics, do research, and write reports. Urge them to read each other's completed reports.

MAKING UP MY MIND

"I'm thinking...Should I raise money to send to Friends of the Earth or write a letter to a senator? Will I join the protest march or make a poster for the Clean Air Project? Do I know how I really feel about these problems?"

— Should we take care of the earth? Of course, it's my home and it's your home, too!

When we need to make up our minds about special concerns, it is important to understand and consider all sides of these issues, both good and bad.

Make a list of important environmental problems in your area.

1. _____
2. _____
3. _____
4. _____

Now, circle the issue you want to think more about, and complete the chart below.

GOOD POINTS

1. _____
2. _____
3. _____

BAD POINTS

1. _____
2. _____
3. _____

After considering all sides of this issue, decide what your action will be. Why?

_____
_____
_____
_____
_____

Name(s) _____

FOR A BETTER WORLD

Environmental problems affect us all. Are there changes that can be made in your life for a better world?

Here's an environmental checklist to follow:

1. Recycle all cans and bottles that are not returnable.
2. Recycle newspapers.
3. Recycle glass jars and bottles.
4. Check plastic for the recyclable symbol and recycle if possible.
5. Make trips to a recycling center when curbside collection is unavailable.
6. Do not use styrofoam products, if possible.
7. Turn off water when soaping hands or brushing teeth.
8. Think about what you want before opening the refrigerator.
9. Turn off the television and lights when not in use.
10. Use writing and drawing paper on both sides.
11. Walk, ride a bicycle, or ride with others to save energy.
12. Make an effort to buy recycled products.
13. Use cloth products instead of plastic when possible.
14. Give reusable toys and clothing to others.
15. Respect the environment and help to preserve wildlife.

List what you already do in the "Super Job" column and what you don't do in the "Uh-Oh" list. Think about this and discuss it with your classmates and family. Make some plans in the "For a Better World" column.

Name(s)_____

MY VIEW/YOUR VIEW

Make an interview mobile to hang in your classroom.
They are fun to make and interesting to read!

Materials needed:
- wire coat hanger
- string
- black construction paper
- scissors
- paper
- note pad

To Do:

1. Choose a current environmental topic and write it as a question. For example, "What do you think about other states bringing their trash to our state's landfills?"
2. Ask four or more people for their responses to your question. Write their responses in the note pad.
3. Cut silhouettes from black paper. Paste a copy of each person's response along with his or her name on each of the silhouettes.
4. Attach the silhouettes to your hanger with pieces of string. Make each silhouette hang at a different length.
5. Add your question to the top of the hanger.
6. Hang it for all to view and read.

Name(s) _____

BE LIGHT RIGHT

Do you realize that every time you turn a light switch on or off you are affecting the environment? According to the World Resources Institute, one-fifth of all electricity used is for lighting, and the more electricity used, the more industrial waste is generated from power plants. Industrial waste is one of the major factors contributing to the greenhouse effect.

Conservation begins with turning off your lights and television when not in use. You can do more for energy conservation by purchasing compact fluorescent light bulbs. These are big energy savers! Here are some facts to consider:

A fluorescent bulb uses about one-fourth of the energy a regular light bulb uses.

A fluorescent bulb lasts about 10,000 hours. That's as long as thirteen regular bulbs!

Each fluorescent light bulb saves enough energy to keep one-half ton of carbon dioxide out of the Earth's atmosphere.

Now, try to solve these problems.

Count how many light bulbs you have in your home. Assume each fluorescent bulb costs $13.75 and each traditional bulb costs $1.00.

1. How much money will it cost to replace the old bulbs in your home with new fluorescent bulbs?
2. What percentage of energy will you save by using fluorescent bulbs?
3. How many tons of carbon dioxide will this keep out of the atmosphere?
4. Do you think this is a good idea? Why?

Name(s)_____

CONSUMER CONTROL

As a consumer, you have a right to know where a company stands regarding environmental issues such as the disposal of toxic waste, air pollution, recycling, processing, packaging, and energy consumption. By asking questions and becoming an informed consumer, you can make a difference in how local businesses treat the environment. You are never too young to make your voice heard!

To Do: Pick a store, restaurant, business, or company whose environmental policy you would like to know more about. Formulate a list of questions you want to ask, and write them in the space below. The next step is to include the questions in a letter and mail the letter to the company you chose.

Name(s) _____

ENVIRONMENTAL TIPS
FOR MOM AND DAD

Your parents have been educating you for years. Now it is time for you to give them some good advice. Try it! Most parents will listen.

Read through this list of conservation suggestions, and then choose a few to include in a "Memo to Mom" or "Data for Dad." Of course, you may add anything else that you've learned about conservation, recycling, and the environment.

SUGGESTIONS

- Urge your company to buy office supplies made from recycled materials.
- Take part in recycling programs at work, or start one of your own.
- At work, use china coffee mugs instead of disposable cups.
- Drive less; walk or ride a bicycle for short-distance trips.
- Check your car's tires. Under-inflated tires cause your car to use more fuel.

- Recycle old motor oil.
- Reduce use of your automobile's air conditioner to help reduce the amount of chlorofluorocarbons (CFCs) in the atmosphere.
- Buy products without excess packaging.
- Use fluorescent light bulbs.
- Replace aerosol sprays with pump sprays.

memo to: _____

from: _____

_____
_____
_____
_____
_____
_____
_____

Name(s)_____

LOOK AT THE SHAPE
WE'RE IN

When writing a poem of your own, you can choose not only the subject matter and words you want, but also where you place the words on the page. Sometimes it can be fun to try to match the shape of a poem with its subject matter.

Write some "shape poems" that contain good advice about conservation. You can choose to rhyme or write in free verse (without rhyme). Be creative and have fun!

example→ • Cover up, don't burn your skin. Protection is what we lack. • Help! we need our ozone is not in} back! Tan is not is not in} back! Sunshines bright.

example→ Giraffe. Tall, long, thin neck. Lots of spots. You need our protection to survive.

Try these ↓

Name(s) _____

JACKET REPORT

Make a book jacket. Choose a topic from the list below, and do some research on it. Don't write a book – just the cover. On the cover, write a summary of the information you discovered in your research.

CONSERVATION TOPICS

- Toxic waste
- Extinction
- Solar energy
- Agriculture
- Recycling
- Water conservation
- Air pollution
- Fossil fuels
- Waste disposal
- Cleaning products
- Rain forests
- Biodegradable products
- Deforestation
- Nuclear energy

I.

Fold this page into four sections along the dotted lines. These folds will divide the page into a long, narrow book cover.

Reverse this page and follow the directions I – IV on each section.

On the reverse side of this section, write the summary of this book (your brief report).

II.

On the reverse side of this section, make a book cover.

Decide on a title. Make it big and bold, then draw a small illustration. Color it bright and beautiful!

III.

The back cover usually tells about the author. (That would be you.)

It also provides some information about the author's qualifications. What kind of research was done to write this book?

Tell it all! A photo or drawing of the author will make it special!

IV.

This section of the book jacket provides a continuation of the book summary.

A small illustration can also be placed in this area.

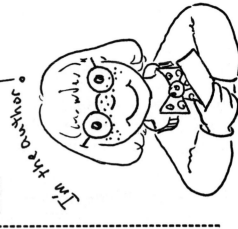

I'm the author!

Name(s)

COOPERATIVE LEARNING BOARDS

Working together in Green Teams can enhance learning. Have each Green Team come up with an idea for an environmental bulletin board. Tell them to design the board to be both eye-catching and informative. Each week, place a different Green Team's design on your classroom bulletin board.

> **Reduce, Reuse, Recycle,**
> **Clean up the Earth today!**
> **You can make a difference.**
> **Do it the Green Team way!**

While the bulletin boards are up, you may also want to set up a temporary recycling collection center in your classroom. Provide each Green Team with a recycling bag. Bring in a bathroom scale. Have students collect items that can be recycled, and weigh the materials each day. Keep track of the results on a graph. You may wish to hold a contest and pick a daily winner for the team that brings in the greatest amount of recyclable items. Use crates, buckets, and boxes for convenient separation.

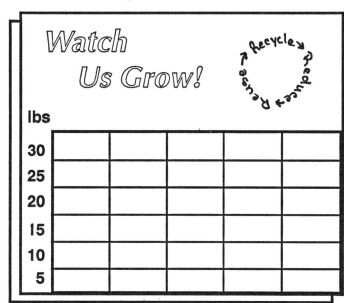

A GREENER VOCABULARY

Each field of study adds new vocabulary words to the language or changes the meaning of existing words. Here is a list of vocabulary words which have special meanings in environmental studies. Some of these words may be new to you, and some you may already know. Review their meanings, then complete one of the following exercises using some of the vocabulary words.

- **Write a brief essay**
- **Devise a word search**
- **Write a rap song**
- **Draw a four-part cartoon or a picture story**

WORD LIST

Strategy	Preservation	Vital	Management	Prestige
Natural	Protection	Habitat	Wildlife	Cooperation
Quality	Ecology	Natural	Awareness	Motivation
Action	Commitment	Challenge	Responsibility	

Name(s)_____

A CALL TO CAUCUS:
ENVIRONMENTAL ABUSE

Provide small groups with the following "trigger topics," and have them brainstorm for research topics.

After topics have been chosen and approved, have each group research its topic, write a report, and prepare a class presentation/discussion of the topic.

ACID RAIN

Many lakes and forests in the northern United States are being destroyed by fossil fuels that pollute the atmosphere. The food chain that birds, fish, and other animals depend upon is also being depleted by acid rain. What causes acid rain? What are its effects? What is being done to halt its effects? What more can be done?

SPRAYS AND PESTICIDES

Pesticides and other toxic substances linger in the environment and threaten the survival of our planet. For years, many species of birds, fish, and other animals have become sick or infertile due to a contaminated food chain. What are pesticides? What effects do pesticides have on the food chain? Can environmental damage due to the use of toxins be reversed? What more can be done to prevent toxins from being used?

WATER POLLUTION

Each year, millions of tons of crude oil are spilled in our rivers and oceans. These spills are mostly accidents; however, our waters have also become unofficial dumping grounds for waste products. Countless birds and other wildlife suffer needless deaths due to the careless destruction of our water sources. How can this be controlled? What are some effective clean-up methods for oil spills?

Name(s) _____

VIEWS AND REVIEWS

When discussing a serious issue, two people may not agree on how to solve the problem, what the causes and effects of the problem are, or whether the issue is a problem at all! For example, some people believe that cutting down the trees where the spotted owl lives is wrong and should be made illegal by the national government. Other people, though, feel that the land should be used to provide timber and jobs for people.

In order for you to become an informed defender of your position, you must understand all sides of the issue in question. Are there people who disagree with your beliefs? Why? If you know what everyone thinks about an issue, you will be better able to defend your own position.

Try This: Look through a magazine or newspaper for an article that discusses a serious environmental problem. Cut out the article, and paste it in the space provided. After reading the article, address the issue from a point of view opposite to your own, and explain how you would solve the problem. Remember, this will not be your real opinion!

paste clipping
here

_____

_____

_____

_____

_____

_____

_____

_____

Name(s)_____

THE SEEDS OF CHANGE: ENVIRONMENTAL ADVOCACY IN ACTION

Protecting the environment is more than just "getting into the spirit" or following a trend. To be effective, conservation must become a lifelong, personal commitment. The children in your classroom are full of hope; they are willing and able to learn what needs to be done to begin cleaning up the Earth. However, we must teach them to go a step beyond this. Not only must they learn how to act on a personal level, but they must become environmental advocates who speak up for their beliefs and who teach others to do the same.

In this chapter, we ask students to reach out to others and let their voices be heard. We've provided role models as examples, and we ask that they become role models for a younger generation of conservationists, as well. As always, group activities are stressed.

SEEDS OF CHANGE: ENVIRONMENTAL ADVOCACY IN ACTION

BIRTHDAY STORY

Interview your grandmother, grandfather, or someone else who has lived a long time. Find out what life was like on his or her fifth birthday, then find out how the world had changed by his or her fiftieth birthday. Make yourself a list of eight to ten specific questions ahead of time. Ask about the state of the environment, natural resources, wildlife, etc. Take your notes on the back of the page, then write a report or summary on the cake.

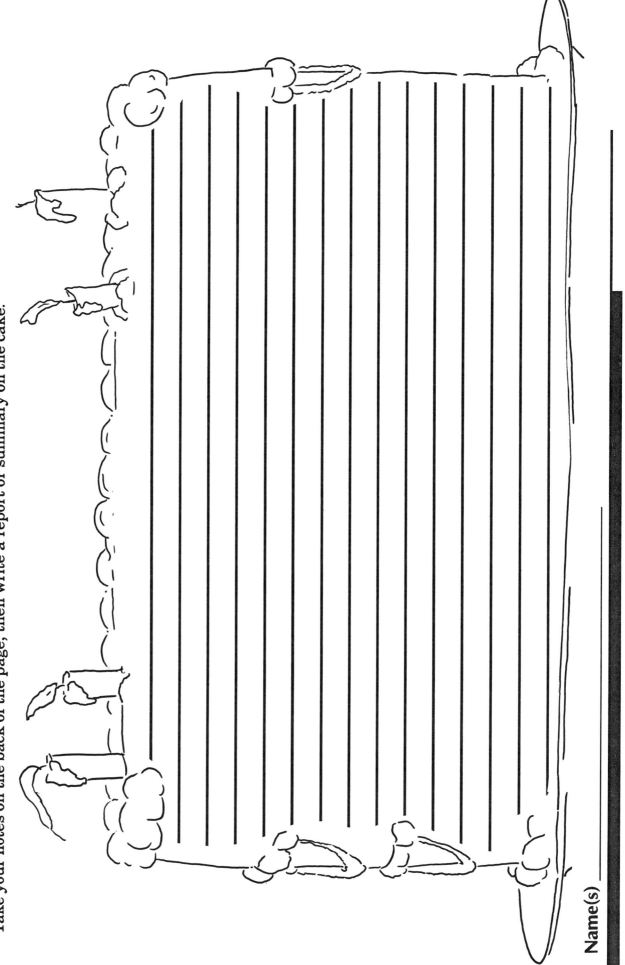

Name(s)

PUPPET POWER

Now that you know quite a bit about conservation and the environment, it is important that you share your knowledge with others. Little kids need to know how to take care of the planet, too. Why not teach them some of what you know? Here's a tip. While little kids will listen if you simply read them a story, you can really grab their attention and help them to remember what you have to say if you put on a puppet show.

To Do:

1. Draw a puppet face on the front of the lunch bag your teacher gives you. Use crayons or construction paper to make the puppet interesting.

2. Write a poem, short story, or just some important facts dealing with conservation and the environment on the back of the bag. Remember, don't make the puppet or the information scary.

3. Make arrangements with your teacher to use your puppet to instruct students in a primary class.

Name(s)_____

Make A Difference

START TODAY

- Reduce
- Reuse
- Recycle

This brochure was made possible by:

_____

_____
Class

_____
School

Thank you for reading it.

MAN OF THE SEA

GREEN TEAM ASSIGNMENT

Captain _____   Date _____

Crew   _____   _____

            _____   _____

Again and again the shark dived for the man. The frightened swimmer waved his arms and blew bubbles in the water. When the shark finally glided right for the man, he hit the shark on its snout with his camera. The frightened shark turned and swam away. The man was Jacques Cousteau.

As a young boy, Jacques loved the sea. He watched boats in the water, then learned to play and swim in the ocean. When he was ten years old, his family moved from France to New York City. "Jack," as he was known in America, became an excellent swimmer when he attended a summer camp in Vermont. He impressed the counselors there by diving deep under the water's surface to clear away tangled branches that were blocking the swimming area. This was just the beginning of a life-long relationship with the water.

When Jacques later returned to France, swimming and inventing became his two favorite hobbies. He eventually joined the French Naval Academy. While recovering from an automobile accident, Jacques tried out his first pair of underwater goggles and became fascinated with the variety of underwater life forms he saw. After World War II, he developed a method for underwater diving using oxygen tanks and later perfected the aqua-lung and the diving saucer.

By 1950, Jacques had bought his own ship, the *Calypso*. Along with scientists, sailors, divers, and members of his own family, Jacques began to explore the sea. He has since written numerous books and documentaries on the beauty and magic of the sea.

Years later, Jacques noticed how badly polluted the oceans were becoming. "All pollution ends up in the sea," he said. In an effort to change this, he formed the Cousteau Society which today works through the United Nations to develop strict worldwide anti-pollution laws. He believes that by working together and speaking out, everyone can help to stop pollution.

To Do: Learn more about Jacques Cousteau and write a Green Team report on his work.

Name(s)_____

COULD WE?

Learning about nature helps us to become better conservationists and take care of our planet. Because this is such a big job, joining together to work as a team can make it a lot easier.

To Do: Think about some of the things you would like to do to help the environment. Plan several activities that require a group contribution. Write a memo to members of your family and friends describing your plans. Send the memo out, get your group together, and choose an activity to complete. Have fun!

Dear:

_____

_____

_____

_____

_____

_____

_____

_____

_____

_____

Name(s) _____

KUDOS TO YOU

A little praise goes a long way to bring out the best in people. Reward your family or friends for their good work helping to clean up the environment. You may also want to reward a local organization or business that is making an effort to practice conservation. For example, you may have noticed that a particular fast food chain has switched from using plastic food containers to paper ones.

To Do: Write a letter telling the person or business of your choice what a good job you feel is being done.

You're super!

Name(s)_____

THE "CAN DO" KIDS

You can draw your own "Can Do" Kid over there.

The "Can Do" Kids are really swell.
They pick up trash and junk that fell.

They've come to say, "Please don't pollute.
Be like us, and give a hoot!"

So much to learn, so much to do,
To help the Earth for me and you.

You know you can do lots of things to protect the environment. How about teaching little kids what you have learned? Let the "Can Do" Kids help you.

1. Color and cut out the "Can Do" Kids. Attach them to paper loops to make finger puppets. You can also paste them onto tongue depressors.
2. Write a poem, story, or just some facts that you have learned about conservation and the environment. Don't forget to give your "Can Do" Kids names!
3. Use your puppets to tell a story to some children in kindergarten or first grade.

Name(s) _____

PROMISES, PROMISES

 TEACHER TIDBIT pg.158

Are you a recycling specialist by now? A master of the wilderness? A conser- vationist with a cause? A wildlife authority? An expert at detecting and eliminating pollution? Do you have a special cause? What will you continue to do, or plan to begin doing, to make a difference in the state of the environment?

In fifty words or less, create a personal pledge to protect the environment. Include tasks you know you are capable of accomplishing.

Promises

_____

_____

_____

_____

_____

_____

_____

_____

_____   _____
date   *signature*

Name(s)_____

PROMISES
BULLETIN BOARD

PURPOSE
To provide a stimulating bulletin board for students to display their achievements and become motivated to do more to protect the environment.

CONSTRUCTION
Back a portion of your bulletin board with brightly colored paper. Make a large ribbon from construction paper. Have a supply of smaller ribbons for daily winners. Cut the title from paper of a contrasting color.

USE
After reading your students' Promises pledges, feature a different student's pledge daily. Present each student with a ribbon to congratulate him or her for conservation efforts.

BUMPER SAYINGS

Bumper stickers are a great way to let your message travel throughout the countryside. Everyone reads them! Take your environmental message to the streets, and design your own bumper sticker. Here's how:

1. Think of several catchy sayings that promote environmental awareness. Use as few words as possible to get your message across.
2. Choose your best slogan. Print it in large letters in the space below.
3. Add color with markers, paint, or crayons.
4. Cut it out.
5. Cover it with clear contact paper or plastic.
6. Ask someone you know to tape it on an automobile's bumper.

Stop Waste.
Slow down Consuming.
Go with Recycling.

Emily, Age 10

Name(s)

HOP TO IT!

I've been hopping to make a difference. Have you?

You know that if you want something to happen you have to make it happen. A good thing takes some effort, but it's always worth it.

What do you want to see happen to your neighborhood's environment? Do you need curbside recycling pickup? Less air pollution? Cleaner drinking water? More use of solar energy? Less toxic waste? What else?

Focus on one of these environmental issues, and make your concerns visible to the general public. Here are some options:

- Make a poster, and send it to someone in a position of power.
- Write a letter expressing your concerns and views. Send it to your legislator, your school and local newspapers, a major corporation, or a community leader. Send a poster with your letter to receive extra attention.

Start your poster here

Name(s) _____

VOICE OF THE EVERGLADES

GREEN TEAM ASSIGNMENT

Captain _____   **Date** _____

Crew _____   _____

_____   _____

In southern Florida, there exists a mysterious world of water and grass called the Everglades. The Everglades is a large ecosystem (4000 square miles) comprising a network of wildlife, water, and weather systems. This area is fragile, however, and is endangered by new dams, drainage systems, and overall mismanagement.

One concerned group called Friends of the Everglades is fighting to save this great natural area from destruction. The group's founder is 92-year-old Marjorie Stoneman Douglas. For more than sixty years, she has worked to protect the Everglades and all its creatures from human development.

Marjorie was born into a Quaker family in Minnesota, and she always felt that her heritage was at the base of her "independence and pig-headedness." As a young woman, she moved to Miami, Florida, to live with her father, Frank Stoneman, who was the owner of the newspaper *The Miami Herald*. It was while working for her father's newspaper that she began her career as a writer and reporter. She also became interested in the debate over the future of an area of land just west of

Miami. Many people wanted to drain the land and use it for development. Marjorie joined the fight to keep the Everglades untouched.

In 1942, Marjorie was asked to write about the Everglades for a series of books on rivers. Because the Everglades is composed of water flowing through Florida's saw grass from Lake Okeechobee toward the Ten Thousand Islands, she called the area the "River of Grass." This name appealed to the citizens of Florida and actually helped to change their minds about the purpose of the Everglades. By 1947, the Florida Everglades was established as a national park protected by the federal government.

Today, the strange jungle-like terrain which houses rare flowers, majestic birds like the heron and the eagle, and exotic animals like the panther and the alligator still needs an advocate against development and pollution. If the wildlife of the Everglades is to endure, new and better conservation programs need to be enacted.

To Do:
1. Look at a map and locate the Florida Everglades. Do some research to learn more about the area.
2. Is there an environmental program in your area that needs help? What can you do close to your home to aid in conservation efforts?

Name(s) _____

THE ADVOCATE

I'm an adva- adva- I'm a defender of the environment!

To be an environmental advocate today is an important role, but, what exactly does being an "advocate" mean? The dictionary defines the noun "advocate" as:

> One who defends;
> One who is committed

The word may also be used as a verb, meaning:

> To plead in favor of;
> To support;
> To urge by agreement

According to these definitions, you are an environmental advocate! You know the problems we must face in the world today, and you also know that we must all work together to make the Earth a place where future generations can live in health and harmony with the environment.

Think of what you have learned about being a good conservationist. Write a sentence whose first letter corresponds to each of the letters in the word advocate describing what you've learned.

A _____

_____

D _____

_____

V _____

_____

O _____

_____

C _____

_____

A _____

_____

T _____

_____

E _____

_____

Name(s) _____

A PLEDGE TO THE ENVIRONMENT

_____

pledges a lifetime commitment to preserving the environment to the best of his or her ability and becoming a responsible and active conservationist. Furthermore, _____ will work to promote environmental awareness in others.

From this day forth, _____ will be an official member of the Green Team.

_____   _____
signature   date

HELPING HANDS:
FUN-FILLED ACTIVITIES TO
PROMOTE CONSERVATION

Much of this book has dealt with serious information on conservation as well as activities to enhance students' critical thinking skills. In this chapter, we suggest a variety of hands-on activities which emphasize the enjoyment of conservation. Kids love to cut, paste, and get their hands dirty. Here are some great opportunities for them to do just that while continuing to learn about the importance of conservation.

We also continue our focus on family activities in this chapter. Make sure some of these exercises are taken home for students to share with their parents, brothers, and sisters.

HELPING HANDS:
FUN-FILLED ACTIVITIES
TO PROMOTE CONSERVATION

RUB IT

Capture the beauty of nature on paper by making a rubbing! This is one way to enjoy your environment all year long, without destroying it.

You Will Need:
- This worksheet
- A crayon of your favorite color
- Something to rub (look for an item with textures)
    - piece of tree trunk
    - pine needles
    - dried grasses, weeds, or petals
    - pebbles

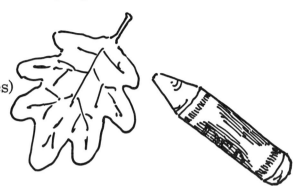

Place the worksheet over the item you wish to rub. Use the side of your crayon for rubbing. Use firm, but gentle, coloring strokes.

Mount or frame your beautiful piece of the world. Tell your classmates about your rubbing.

Name(s) _____

RECYCLE YOUR OWN PAPER!

Have students work in teams to produce their own recycled paper. You may want to try this first yourself.

You Will Need:
- A 9 1/2" by 10" piece of wire screen. (Ask parents to supply or buy scraps from hardware store.)
- Egg-beater
- Mixing spoon
- Measuring cup
- Old newspapers
- Water
- Starch
- Flat pan (cookie sheet with sides or a baking pan larger than the screen)
- Large bowl

Process:
1. Tear sheet of newspaper into small pieces. Place in bowl.
2. Cover with water and allow to soak at least one hour.
3. Mix with hands, then beat with egg-beater until mushy. If the mixture is too thick, add more water.
4. Mix two tablespoons of corn starch with one cup of water.
5. Stir the cornstarch mixture into the pulp (wet paper mixture).
6. Pour pulp into pan.
7. Place the piece of screen in the pan, and use your fingers to cover it with pulp.
8. Spread several pages of newspaper on a flat area.
9. Carefully remove screen from pan; place the screen along with recycled paper mixture on newspaper to blot dry.
10. Fold the paper over, and press on it to remove any excess moisture.
11. Open the paper, and allow it to dry completely.
12. The next day, slowly pull the recycled paper from the screen.

MOMENTOUS MONTAGE

A montage is a collection of pictures or images which are placed together to make a whole. You can create a montage to tell a story about the environment.

You Will Need:

- Magazines or newspapers
- Piece of cardboard
- Scissors and glue
- A theme or storyline to follow

To Do: As you look through a magazine, think about your world and all that is happening in it. Come up with a theme you wish to present (such as "wasteful products," "cleaning up our oceans," or "saving the elephant"). Cut out magazine pictures which match the topic you have chosen. As you cut out your pictures, give them unusual shapes and angles. Finally, fill out the montage description sheet with your name, the title of your work, and a brief description. Paste your montage and description sheet onto the piece of cardboard. Remember to overlap the edges of your pictures. Use your imagination!

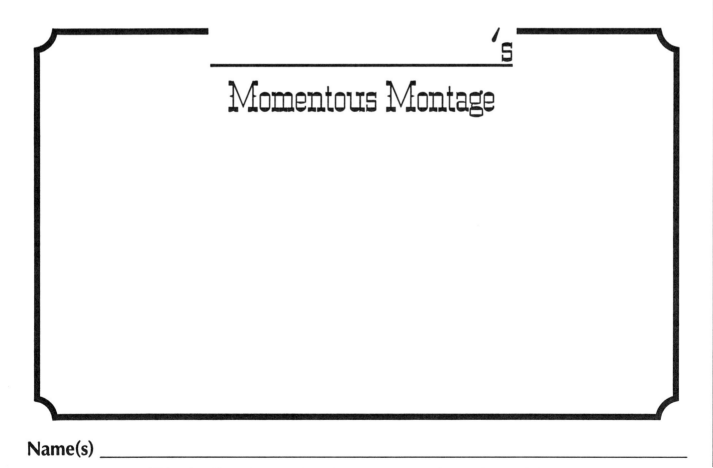

_____'s

Momentous Montage

Name(s) _____

BIG SPRING RACE

Watching plants grow can be a great deal of fun. It can be especially fun if you and a partner grow plants together. Because different seeds grow at different rates, you can have a Spring Plant Race with your partner.

You Will Need:
- Six different seeds
- Plastic egg carton
- Water
- A friend

To Do:
1. Cut your egg container in half.
2. Dampen the soil.
3. Poke a pencil in the soil. Plant one seed in each cup, and gently cover each seed with soil.
4. Place your seeds in the sun, and watch them grow.
5. Each day, add one teaspoon of water to the soil.
6. Keep a growth record on the chart. Check the germination estimates on the package, and compare with how quickly your plant grows.
7. Compare your plant's growth with that of your friend's plant.

Seeds	Day sprouted	1" tall	2" tall
1.			
2.			
3.			
4.			
5.			
6.			

Name(s) _____

GARDEN MAGIC

Be a complete recycler by composting your kitchen and garden waste. (Compost is a mixture of organic materials which are aged and then used as fertilizer.) Here's how to do it:

Step One: Choose an out-of-the-way spot in your yard that is level and exposed to a great deal of sun. You may want to dig a hole for your compost, or you can place a fence around the area to protect it from animals.

Step Two: Keep a container under your kitchen sink to collect fruit and vegetable scraps and peelings. Do not include any meat or bones.

Step Three: Make layers of the kitchen waste, yard trimmings, and dirt in your compost heap outside. Sprinkle the heap with water and turn it over every few days to keep it light and fluffy.

Step Four: The compost should remain in your yard for about two months. Once ready, the composted material can be used as fertilizer for your garden. You can begin a second compost heap in a nearby area.

Name(s) _____

WHEEL OF TROUBLE

Loggerhead sea turtles are in danger of becoming extinct as people continue to hunt them for their shells, eggs, and meat. These turtles are also needlessly killed by shrimp nets in the ocean. As the nets are thrown into the sea to pick up shrimp, many turtles find themselves caught in the nets and unable to escape. The turtle population is also affected by water pollution and natural predators such as possums and raccoons.

By alerting people to this growing problem, you can help the sea turtles survive. Make a paper turtle to show your family and friends what is happening.

You Will Need:
- Two paper plates
- Green construction paper
- Brass fastener
- Markers and glue

PROBLEMS:
Natural predators
(possums and raccoons)
Over-harvesting
Development of beach areas
Water pollution
Shrimp nets

To Construct:
1. Divide one plate into four sections to make the body of the turtle.
2. Draw a picture on each section showing a problem the turtle faces. You may choose to write a descriptive sentence in each section instead.
3. Cut out a head, four legs, and a tail and paste them to the body.
4. Cover the top of the other plate with green paper to make the turtle shell.
5. Cut out one section of the second plate equal to the area of the body.
6. Make designs on the shell.
7. Attach the shell to the body with the fastener.

Show your friends and family the turtle, and alert them to its problems.

More: Can you design a wheel of trouble for another animal in danger?

Name(s)_____

MINI ECOSPHERE

A well-balanced ecosphere can be created inside your own home with the proper amounts of water, soil, and plants. You can build a terrarium to house the environment from items found in and around your home. Here's how.

You Will Need:
- A container (wide-mouthed glass jar with lid, plastic shoe box with lid, an aquarium, or any clear container covered with plastic wrap and rubber band)
- Sand or pebbles
- A few small pieces of charcoal
- Soil and a few rocks
- Small plants from the woods (use plants that do not grow too tall, such as moss, lichens, and tiny ferns)
- Long-handled planting tools

Process:
1. Place sand and pebbles in the bottom of your container.
2. Add small bits of charcoal.
3. Put down a layer of soil.
4. Carefully place your plants in the soil.
5. Arrange the rocks around the container.
6. Water the terrarium until the soil is slightly moist. Do not overwater.
7. Cover the container, and place in a cool area with indirect sunlight.

If you overwater the soil, mold or mildew may appear. Let the terrarium dry uncovered for a day, then begin again.

It's the perfect size for me!

Name(s) _____

EATING GREEN

Most people buy their food from the grocery store. It can be fun, though, to grow your own food. Here's an item you can grow in your kitchen and enjoy on salads and sandwiches...Bean sprouts!

You Will Need:
- Seeds (two tablespoons of alfalfa, or one-half cup of mung beans or lentils)
- Quart jar
- Thin piece of cloth for top
- Rubber band

Process:
This will take approximately five days.

Day One
1. Wash seeds or beans.
2. Place in jar.
3. Cover with water, and soak overnight.

Day Two
1. In the morning, drain off water through the cloth.
2. Rinse with fresh water.
3. Drain seeds again. The seeds must remain damp, however.
4. Prop jar on its side to drain. Place it in an area the receives indirect light.
5. Rinse and drain seeds once again.

Days Three to Five
1. Rinse and drain seeds twice a day.

TIP - *Alfalfa sprouts will turn a beautiful green if you put them in the sun for at least two days.*

The beans are ready when:
Alfalfa beans have sprouted between one and two inches long.
Mung beans have sprouted between one and one-half and two and one-half inches long.
Lentil beans have sprouted to one inch.

Name(s)_____

AN ALL-SEASON
NATURE WREATH

Remember Henry David Thoreau's words:
  "It is the marriage of the soul with nature that gives birth to the imagination."

Nature walks are enjoyable at any time of
the year. On these walks, you can try to
identify birds and wildflowers. You may
catch a glimpse of wild animals or their
tracks. Next time you're on a nature walk,
gather up items to make a wreath to
remember nature by.

Do not disturb living things on your walk. Instead, look on the ground for small
items to glue onto your wreath such as dried weeds, wildflowers, leaves, moss,
acorns, pine cones, feathers, and pretty pebbles. When you return home you can
begin to design your wreath.

You Will Need:
- A flat piece of cardboard
- Scissors
- Glue
- Florist's wire
- Ribbon for a bow

Cut the cardboard into the shape of a
wreath, and glue the items you found onto
the wreath. Design a bow with the ribbon,
and tie it to the wreath with the florist's
wire. Be as creative as you can!

Name(s) _____

BIRD FEEDERS GALORE

Bird watching can be a great winter activity. One way to make sure the birds visit your house is to set up a bird feeder in your own backyard. You can make a bird feeder yourself using items found around your house!

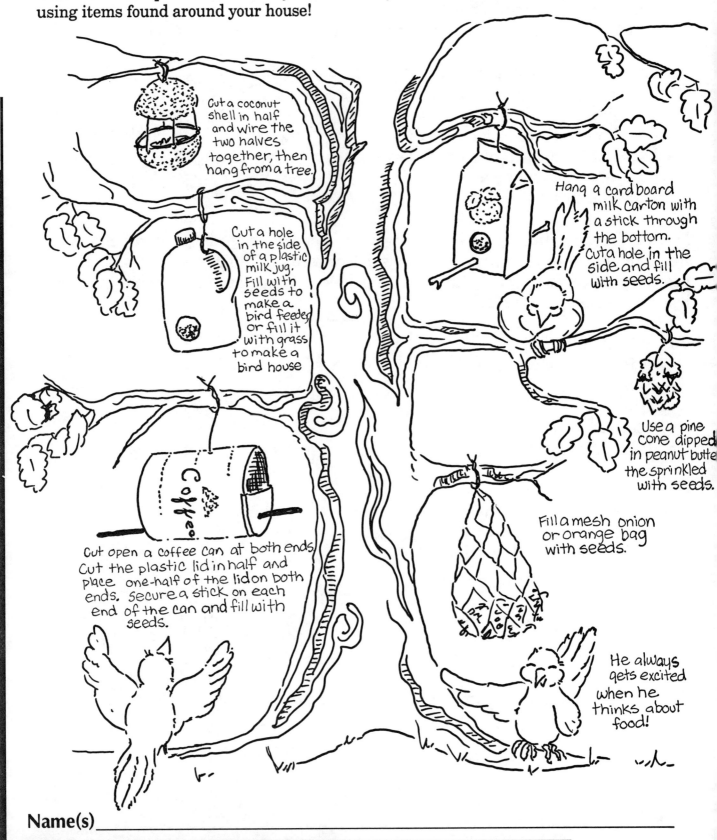

Cut a coconut shell in half and wire the two halves together, then hang from a tree.

Cut a hole in the side of a plastic milk jug. Fill with seeds to make a bird feeder or fill it with grass to make a bird house

Hang a cardboard milk carton with a stick through the bottom. Cut a hole in the side and fill with seeds.

Use a pine cone dipped in peanut butter the sprinkled with seeds.

Cut open a coffee can at both ends. Cut the plastic lid in half and place one-half of the lid on both ends. Secure a stick on each end of the can and fill with seeds.

Fill a mesh onion or orange bag with seeds.

He always gets excited when he thinks about food!

Name(s) _____

CRITTER CRAFTS

Let our animal friends hang out around the classroom or in your home to remind you how special each animal is.

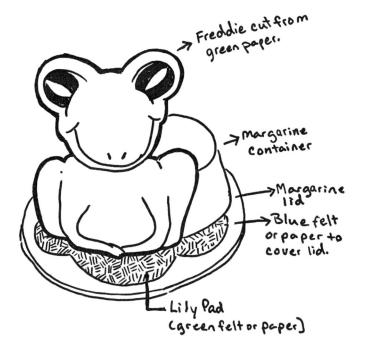

→ Freddie cut from green paper.

→ Margarine container

→ Margarine lid

→ Blue felt or paper to cover lid.

⌐ Lily Pad (green felt or paper)

Freddy Frog Paper Clip Holder
All you need is a clean margarine container with lid, blue and green felt or construction paper, glue, and colored markers.

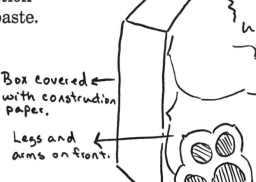

Blacky's head ↑ coming up from middle of box.

→ Corners trimmed off detergent box.

Box covered ← with construction paper.

Legs and ← arms on front.

Blacky Bear Magazine Holder
Get an empty, sturdy detergent box. Cut it open at the top and cut both sides at an angle, as illustrated. You will also need brown construction paper, colored markers, and paste.

Name(s) _____

ENERGY HOUNDS

Did you know that lighting accounts for twenty percent of all electricity used in the United States? Try to reduce the use of electricity in your home by placing reminders in all the rooms. The energy hound will keep constant watch to be sure that everyone is saving electricity.

To Do: Cut cardboard to fit one of the patterns below, then decorate it with your own energy hound. Write a simple reminder on the plate. Take it home, and place it near the light switch in your living room or kitchen.

Name(s)_____

THE ULTIMATE TEACHER

Congratulations! You are the ultimate teacher, helping your students develop a sense of responsibility and commitment to the environment. This final chapter provides suggestions on methods of implementing and expanding the activities presented in this manual. Feel free to change any of the activities to meet your classroom need, whether it be for level of difficulty, class interest, or time restrictions.

Remember, the information and activities provided in *The Green Team* stress local environmental issues over national and global ones. While it is important for young people to be aware of what is occurring worldwide, it is also imperative that we not overwhelm them. Many of the local issues addressed here can be solved, or at least affected, by your students' actions. A successful anti-litter campaign, for example, can engender optimism about a young person's impact on his or her world. As teachers, it is this optimism that we hope to foster in our students as they prepare to take on the responsibilities of adulthood.

THE ULTIMATE TEACHER

T-E-A-M: GREEN TEAM

Green Team activity sheets are scattered throughout this book. We focus on teamwork because we feel it improves learning through the dynamics of dialogue and discussion. When working together, students achieve more and have more fun. The team process is a unique phenomenon which enables the team members to achieve momentum and motivation. These factors are especially important when studying the environment, as the problems faced are so large. Having fun and making an impact at an early age may help students to become life-long environmental advocates.

The process used to implement your Green Teams should reflect the atmosphere of your classroom and your individual teaching style. You may want to adapt some or all of the following methods to help you get your group work going.

1. Make use of Green Teams for at least half of the school year. You may need to rearrange team make-up if intra-group problems arise.
2. Mix the ability and attention-span levels of group members. Keep the groups to between five and seven students.
3. Have group members vote to select a captain. Change captains every month to allow each student an opportunity to serve. Groups should elect students for additional jobs, such as secretary, reporter, materials supervisor, etc.
4. Have each member vote to choose a group name.
5. If grades are given for a team activity, all members should receive the same grade, regardless of input.
6. Oversee group activity to ensure that all members share the work load.
7. Encourage all members to participate in dialogues; however, no member should be penalized for remaining silent.
8. Emphasize the importance of good listening skills.
9. The following guidelines are effective when beginning a group activity sheet:
    a. All members read sheets silently.
    b. Each sheet is then read aloud.
    c. Captain initiates and guides discussion.
10. You may want to reserve time to meet with all team captains. Stress the importance of the role and review steps for management.

Remember, the team process can be an important element of your entire classroom program.

ONE-LINERS

Here are some mini-ideas which can be developed into complete lessons.

OUTDOOR ADVENTURE

Using the word "adventure" can add intrigue to a trip to a pond or park. You may also want to visit a wildlife refuge or local SPCA. Other nature adventures include a cloud walk, a senses walk, and a pollution pick-up.

CLEAN WEEK

Sponsor a school clean-up week.

SIT HIGH AND DRY

Make "sit-upons" prior to an outdoor activity.

FOOD CHAIN HANG-UPS

Make paper loop chains as visual representations of food chains.

ADOPT-A-_____

Decide what needs doing in your community and enlist students to help (eg. beach, park trail, waterfront, school clean-up).

CONSERVATION HOTLINE BULLETIN BOARD

Call the National Wildlife Federation (202/797-6655) for the latest environmental news and display daily or weekly.

FANTASY WALL

Have students make a talking mural, telling how the Earth should be treated.

MAN ON THE STREET

Tape brief interviews on specific environmental issues.

JUNK FOR PROFIT

Have students collect and sell recyclable materials; cash can be sent to an environmental group of your students' choice.

NATIONAL YOUTH SERVICE DAY

Plan a project for this day, which is usually held near the end of April. For more information, write to: National Youth Service Day, c/o Youth Service America, 1319 F Street NW, Washington, D.C. 20004.

STAR SERVE

Find out about this nonprofit organization funded by Kraft General Foods Foundation. It supports various youth service projects. Write to: Star Serve, P.O. Box 34567, Washington, D.C. 20043.

THE NATIONAL WILDLIFE FEDERATION

The National Wildlife Federation and its state affiliates will supply teachers with education kits to celebrate National Wildlife Week (week of April 22). The kits have a different theme each year. Past themes have included endangered species, Earth Day, trees, and the fragile polar regions. The kits contain a 16-page educator's guide, a theme poster, a 12-picture poster, a sheet of Wildlife Stamps, and an Educational Materials Flyer. To obtain a kit, teachers should write to their National Wildlife Federation state affiliate.

Alabama Wildlife Federation
46 Commerce St., P.O. Box 2102
Montgomery, AL 36102

Wildlife Federation of Alaska
750 W. Second Ave., Suite 200-B
Anchorage, AK 99501

Arizona Wildlife Federation
644 N. Country Club, Suite E
Mesa, AZ 85201-4991

Arkansas Wildlife Federation
7509 Cantrell Rd., #104
Little Rock, AR 72207

Golden State Wildlife Federation
2530 San Pablo Ave., Suite D
Berkeley, CA 94702

Colorado Wildlife Federation
7475 Dakin St., Suite 137
Denver, CO 80221

Connecticut Forest and Park Association
Middlefield, 16 Meriden Rd.
Rockfall, CT 06481

Wildlife Federation of Delaware
P.O. Box 8111
Newark, DE 19711

Florida Wildlife Federation
P.O. Box 6870
Tallahassee, FL 32314

Georgia Wildlife Federation
1936 Iris Drive, Suite G
Conyers, GA 30207-5046

Conservation Council for Hawaii
Box 2923
Honolulu, HI 96802

Idaho Wildlife Federation
751 Centro Drive
Twin Falls, ID 83301

Illinois Wildlife Federation
123 S. Chicago Street
Rossville, IL 60963

Indiana Wildlife Federation
301 E. Carmel Dr., Suite G-200
Carmel, IN 46032

Iowa Wildlife Federation
3125 Douglas, Suite 103
Des Moines, IA 50310

Kansas Wildlife Federation
P.O. Box 5715
Topeka, KS 66605

League of Kentucky Sportsmen
P.O. Box 406
Pt. Thomas, KY 41075

Louisiana Wildlife Federation
337 S. Acadian Throughway
Baton Rouge, LA 70806

Natural Resources Council of Maine
271 State Street
Augusta, ME 04330

Conservation Federation of Maryland
P.O. Box 15336
Chevy Chase, MD 20815

Massachusetts Wildlife Federation
P.O. Box 188
Concord, MA 01742

Michigan United Conservation Clubs, Inc.
2101 Wood Street, Box 30235
Lansing, MI 48909

Minnesota Conservation Federation
1036-B Cleveland Ave.
St. Paul, MN 55116

Mississippi Wildlife Federation
P.O. Box 1814
Jackson, MS 39215-1814

Conservation Federation of Missouri
728 W. Main Street
Jefferson City, MO 65101-1543

Montana Wildlife Federation
P.O. Box 6537
Bozeman, MT 59715

Nebraska Wildlife Federation, Inc.
P.O. Box 81437
Lincoln, NE 68501-1437

Nevada Wildlife Federation, Inc.
P.O. Box 71238
Reno, NV 89570

New Hampshire Wildlife Federation
54 Portsmouth St., Box 239
Concord, NH 03301

New Jersey State Federation of Sportsmen's Clubs
P.O. Box 673
Flanders, NJ 07836

New Mexico Wildlife Federation
3240-D Juan Tabo, N.E., Suite 10
Albuquerque, NM 87111

New York: Vacant
Write to:
National Wildlife Federation
1400 Sixteenth St., N.W.
Washington, D.C. 20036-2266

North Carolina Wildlife Federation
Box 10626
Raleigh, NC 27605

North Dakota Wildlife Federation
P.O. Box 7248
Bismarck, ND 58502

League of Ohio Sportsmen
3953 Indianola Ave.
Columbus, OH 43214

Oklahoma Wildlife Federation
3900 N. Santa Fe Ave.
Oklahoma City, OK 73118

Oregon Wildlife Federation
P.O. Box 67020
Portland, OR 97267

Pennsylvania Federation of Sportsmen's Clubs, Inc.
2426 N. Second St.
Harrisburg, PA 17110

Natural History Society of Puerto Rico, Inc.
GPO Box 1036
San Juan, PR 00936

Environmental Council of Rhode Island, Inc.
P.O. Box 8765
Cranston, RI 02920

South Carolina Wildlife Federation
P.O. Box 61159
Columbia, SC 29260-1159

South Dakota Wildlife Federation
812 N. Monroe
Pierre, SD 57501

Tennessee Conservation League
300 Orlando Ave.
Nashville, TN 37209-3200

Sportsmen Conservationists of Texas
311 Vaughn Bldg., 807 Brazos St.
Austin, TX 78701

Utah Wildlife Federation
Box 65636
Salt Lake City, UT 84165

Vermont Natural Resources Council
9 Bailey Ave.
Montpelier, VT 05602

Virginia Wildlife Federation
4602D W. Grove Ct.
Virginia Beach, VA 23455

Virgin Islands Conservation Society, Inc.
P.O. Box 3839
St. Croix, VI 00822

Washington Wildlife Federation
Rt. 2, Box 195
Pullman, WA 99163

West Virginia Wildlife Federation
Box 275
Paden City, WV 26159

Wisconsin Wildlife Federation, Inc.
Tranquil Acres
Reeseville, WI 53579

Wyoming Wildlife Federation
P.O. Box 106
Cheyenne, WY 82003

MAIL CALL

Make resource lists available for student writing activities. Encourage individual or team letter writing to present a position, ask a question, or gather information.

Environmental Protection Agency Regional Offices:

EPA Region 1
JFK Federal Building
Boston, MA 02203
617/565-3234

EPA Region 2
26 Federal Plaza
New York, NY 10278
212/264-4418

EPA Region 3
841 Chestnut Street
Philadelphia, PA 19107
215/597-4048

EPA Region 4
345 Courtland Street, NE
Atlanta, GA 30365
404/347-2904

EPA Region 5
230 S. Dearborn Street
Chicago, IL 60604
312/886-6165

EPA Region 6
1445 Ross Avenue
Dallas, TX 75202-2733
214/655-7208

EPA Region 7
726 Minnesota Avenue
Kansas City, KS 66101
913/236-2893

EPA Region 8
999 18th Street
One Denver Place,
Suite 1300
Denver, CO
303/293-1648

EPA Region 9
215 Fremont Street
San Francisco, CA 94105
415/974-8378

EPA Region 10
1200 Sixth Avenue
Seattle, WA 98101
206/442-7660

Other Environmental Agencies:

American Forestry
Association
919 17th Street NW
Washington, D.C. 20006

Friends of the Earth
30 E. 42nd Street
New York, NY 10017

National Audubon Society
950 3rd Avenue
New York, NY 10022

National Geographic
Society
17th and M Street, NW
Washington, D.C. 20036

Wilderness Society
729 15th Street, NW
Washington, D.C. 20005

Animal Welfare Institute
P.O. Box 3492
Grand Central Station
New York, NY 10017

The Nature Conservancy
1815 N. Lynn Street
Arlington, VA 22209

HIAWATHA'S BROTHERS, PAGE 11

Explain to your students that Hiawatha was a mythical person sent to the North American Indians to teach them the art of peace, and love for their forests and rivers. This legend was given literary form by the American poet Henry Wadsworth Longfellow.

The short version of "Hiawatha's Childhood" provides a good introduction to this early environmentalist. A slow, second reading may be necessary in order for students to write their lists! Combine individual lists to make a class list and discuss.

ADOPT-A-TREE, PAGE 14

If trees are not plentiful in your area, you may want to take your class on a trip to a wooded area. If possible, encourage snapshots or drawings of trees. I suggest you collect the drawings between seasons to avoid lost or damaged worksheets. A class mural would make a great culminating activity.

THIS IS FOR THE BIRDS, PAGE 20

ACROSS	DOWN
1. Stork	Turkey
2. Roadrunner	Pelican
3. Bald eagle	Flamingo
4. Peacock	Catbird
5. Crow	Chicken
6. Duckling	Dove
7. Robin	Raven
8. Vulture	Owl
9. Pigeon	Penguin
10. Hummingbird	Bob

SHORE LIFE/PLAINS LIFE, PAGE 23

You may want to discuss the basic differences between the two environments before beginning the exercise. Allow time for students to share experiences and opinions.

OUTDOOR PUZZLES, PAGE 25

In order to generate ideas in the classroom, you may want to brainstorm a class list of favorite outdoor things. Students can then make personal lists and word mazes. Exchange completed student puzzles within the classroom.

LEARN-A-LEAF, PAGE 26

You may want to take your class on a walk to select leaves. Remind them to pick the leaves carefully so that branches are not damaged. If possible, provide a tree identification book for student use.

Briefly compare two leaves, noting the similarities and differences for the students. Encourage students to touch items with your supervision. Have students exchange their written descriptions. Spread the leaves out on a table, and have students locate the leaves according to the written description.

*Note - You may find this activity more manageable in small groups.

A NEIGHBOR TO NATURE, PAGE 30

You may want to read aloud excerpts from Thoreau's writing. Many of his quotations are simple and will provide provocative discussions.

In order to provide students with ordinary objects to observe, take a walk in your school yard or a nearby park.

THE PLANT DOCTOR, PAGE 32

Be sure you make available multiple copies of books and materials about George Washington Carver. You may want to read the story aloud and have students take notes. Then, have them write the rest of the story. This will test their note-taking skills.

GREEN VOCABULARY, PAGE 43

To ensure understanding of these terms, use them frequently in a variety of class activities (eg., bulletin board, story starters, posters, etc.). You may have some of your own vocabulary words to add to the list! Encourage students with writing difficulties to make a cassette to aid their memories.

KNOW THE FACTS, PAGE 44

Use this worksheet as a quick check on environmental awareness. It would be a good idea to review the Family List in the classroom prior to having the students take it home. Encourage families to make use of the list to be written on the back of the worksheet. The students could also hang duplicate copies of the list on their refrigerators at home to serve as a friendly reminder.

Student List answers: 1. False 2. True 3. False 4. False 5. True 6. False
Family List answers: 1. True 2. True 3. False 4. False 5. True 6. Answer will vary 7. True 8. True

A GLOBAL PERSPECTIVE, PAGE 50

It may be helpful to review various forms of graphing with your class. Pictographs are especially fun. Be sure to provide a few for practice first. The figures used in this activity are from an Earth Summit report published in *USA Today* on June 2, 1992. Update information if possible.

WHAT'S MOST IMPORTANT?, PAGE 51

Prior to using this worksheet, we suggest that you discuss with your students this list of concepts and terms. Ask students to help provide the definitions. Post a simple list for all to see. Include any other terms you think would be helpful.

Waste dumping: The United States generates 240 million metric tons of hazardous waste annually, all of which goes into underground storage, landfills, rivers, or sewers.

Endangered species: By the year 2050, half the species of plants and animals now alive could be extinct.

Air pollution: Pollutants in the air can create acid that damages lakes and forests and harms humans and animal life.

Clean drinking water: Our drinking water is threatened by contamination from toxic materials in the soil.

Overpopulation: The Earth's population has increased by one billion people over the past ten years. It is estimated that twelve billion people could live on the Earth by the year 2010.

Ozone layer: This protective layer stretches more than ten miles into the Earth's atmosphere and blocks much of the sun's radiation. It is currently being destroyed by artificial substances.

Global warming: "Greenhouse" gases maintain the Earth's life-sustaining temperatures; adding gases like carbon dioxide to the atmosphere causes the temperature to rise.

Rain forests: Destroying the tropical rain forests adds carbon dioxide to the atmosphere.

Fishing grounds: Some fishing areas have been overworked or polluted and must be closed to the public.

Natural resources: Our resources are being depleted due to increased population. New energy sources and building materials must be found.

SNOW BIRDS FLY SOUTH, PAGE 52

Provide 3" by 5" index cards for game questions. You may want to use spelling words, math facts, environmental facts, etc. as game questions. Provide the information, and ask students to write the cards. Students may also want to make up a set of their own questions. You can mount one game board and protect it with lamination, or make individual copies.

MOTHER EARTH'S WORD, PAGE 62

a	r	w	j	i	l	n	b	a	t	t	l	e	s
p	l	o	g	g	e	r	h	e	a	d	t	t	s
r	p	o	z	d	f	l	r	z	m	s	u	n	l
o	b	d	g	h	i	w	n	o	p	q	r	a	d
t	w	s	a	l	m	o	n	e	k	n	t	x	q
e	v	t	j	c	t	s	c	k	w	o	l	f	t
c	l	o	a	d	o	i	w	s	i	b	e	r	u
t	c	r	a	n	e	d	a	v	l	i	d	m	e
i	m	k	s	s	t	e	v	s	d	i	d	w	n
o	o	e	r	o	p	e	f	i	l	c	u	m	b
n	r	o	e	r	o	p	e	s	t	w	o	e	r

UPDATE: MYTHS OR FACTS, PAGE 68

1. Fact	2. Myth
3. Fact	4. Myth
5. Fact	6. Myth
7. Fact	8. Myth
9. Myth	10. Myth

ECO-TRIP, PAGE 71

This form can become part of a class trip booklet or used for an independent exercise. If a class trip is not feasible, perhaps it could be included in a parent-packet to be used on a weekend or during summer vacation.

THE CHASING ARROWS, PAGE 75

Encourage your students to learn as much as they can about recycling. Perhaps you can plan a trip to a recycling center. Writing letters to local industries is a good means of consciousness-raising. You may want to set up a recycling collection center in your classroom or school cafeteria.

BE A ONE TON FAMILY, PAGE 80

Ask students to compare their charts with those of their Green Team partners. Ask for volunteers to share results with the class. Be sure that students know when, or if, they have curbside recycling pick-up. Also find out where the nearest recycling center is. Work with students to come up with solutions to problems that may arise from calls or letters to town officials. The next step is to find out what happens to the recycled newspapers. Is there a market for them? Are they actually being utilized? Find out!

TEACHER TIDBITS

RECYCLED WORDS, PAGE 82

You may wish to make up your own maze and substitute easier words for primary grade students.

VOICE OF THE CONSUMER, PAGE 83

Students may feel more comfortable during an interview if they have a chance to practice first. Provide time for mock interviews. Reinforce the five steps provided on the worksheet. Practice reading the questions may also be beneficial for some students.

Carefully review the Consumer Interview sheet (page 84) with your class. Be sure that students know all the words and terms mentioned in the interview. You may want to clarify the definition of composting. Note that composting is not usually possible in cities. Also mention that only organic items such as yard clippings, vegetable and fruit peelings, and nut shells are normally saved. Meat and bones are not composted.

Also explain that plastic plates are less desirable to use than paper plates as plastics are made from petroleum products that pollute the environment.

Interview teams comprised of two students is a good way to expedite this activity; have one student ask questions and one record responses. It is important to note that the interview serves a dual purpose: it gathers information and raises the awareness of all participants.

TO THE DUMP, PAGE 85

Before using this activity, explain to your class that not all communities recycle or collect all recyclable materials. You may want to plan a trip to the nearest recycling center. Have students share their answers with classmates or Green Team members. Ask them to collaborate on information prior to providing them with the answers.

Answers (not the same for all communities):
1. D 2. C   3. B 4. A 5. A 6. D 7. D 8. D 9. A 10. A
11. A 12. A   13. D 14. B 15. D 16. D 17. D 18. D 19. A 20. A

ARBOR DAY ANY DAY, PAGE 90

The tree planting chart was provided by Global Releaf. For more information about tree planting and care, you can contact Global Releaf at the American Forestry Association, P.O. Box 2000, Washington, D.C. 20013-2000.

GROUP GOALS, PAGE 93

You may want to reproduce the six-step plan on chart paper and demonstrate its effectiveness to the entire classroom. Encourage Green Teams to follow the format.

SHARE THE FACTS, PAGE 94

Ask students to read their written responses aloud. Discuss the various choices made. Be sure to provide the following facts about the different choices:

Choice One - Paper depends on trees which can be replanted. Plastic is made with nonrenewable natural gas and petroleum.

Choice Two - The average person uses about sixty gallons of water daily; about forty percent of that water is wasted. Ten gallons of water per year can be saved by turning off the spigot while you brush your teeth.

Choice Three - Disposable diapers take five hundred years to decompose. The average baby will use more than seven thousand diapers.

THE CAN OF TUNA, PAGE 97

Explain to your students that unless businesses in America make changes in their daily practices, we are not going to make a difference in the environment's condition. Urge students to write letters to major corporations to find out what changes they have made to help the environment.

A Kid's View, page **98**

A wide variety of statements can be added to these sentences. These are just a few examples.

1. Loss of habitat is due to pollution, growth of cities, and global changes.
2. Plants provide food for plant-eating animals which are eaten by meat-eaters; their bodies return minerals to the Earth after they die.
3. Rain forests remove thousands of tons of carbon dioxide from the air.
4. Many new grains depend on fertilizer and pesticides to survive; many breeds of cattle need vaccinations to protect them from diseases and cannot live in the wild.
5. Sewage and garbage-dumping, nuclear wastes, and oil spills are all threats to the world's oceans. Irresponsible dumping in the oceans causes medical and personal waste products to float to shore.
6. Toxic elements in the air are destroying the Earth's ozone layer which is needed to protect the Earth from the sun's harmful rays.

Jacket Report, page **108**

Book jackets can be folded and tacked to a bulletin board for easy reading. You may want to staple a few blank pages inside the jacket to make a slim book. An average-size book jacket can be made by transferring this process to a piece of 8 1/2" by 20" construction paper.

A Call to Caucus: Environmental Abuse, page **111**

A great activity for Green Teams! They can either use one of the topics listed or come up with topics of their own choosing. Topics may also be used as a focus for debating teams. Invite other classes to listen in or join your debate.

Make a Difference Brochure, page **117**

You may want to review what students know about conservation. Stress the Three R's: Reduce, Reuse, and Recycle. Make a class list based upon the discussion. Students will use this information to develop a brochure. Urge them to design an interesting format for this work and add color to the front for extra excitement and interest. Completed brochures should be taken home and shared with the family.

Option: Select one brochure to reproduce; have students give them out at a school or public function. Send a copy to your local newspaper or legislator.

PROMISES, PROMISES, PAGE 122

Other teachers may want to work with you on this project. Set up a review team to judge the winners and stimulate interest in potential competitors. A good way to end the school year!

THE ADVOCATE, PAGE 127

The words commitment and advocate are strong ones and worthy of discussion. It is important to note that the quality of life on this planet can improve only through the understanding and commitment of environmental advocates. You may want to use these words as story-starters or triggers for discussion. Don't let them go to waste.

A PLEDGE TO THE ENVIRONMENT, PAGE 128

Be sure that these awards are given out for significant work or commitment. You can give them to your students and/or they can give them to business or service people who have shown exemplary service to the community, nation, or world.

AN ALL-SEASON NATURE WREATH, PAGE 139

On a different occasion, you may want to make a "junk wreath." Collect litter on your walk, and make wreaths to hang in your school corridor. Post an insert in the center for anti-litter essays.

RESOURCES

Countless resources were utilized in the writing of this book. Many of the statistics, trends, and specific information came from the following sources:

BOOKS

Capone, Lisa and Cady Goldfield. *The Conservationworks Book*. Boston, MA: Appalachian Mountain Club Books, 1992

Carson, Rachel. *The Sea Around Us*. New York, NY: Oxford University Press, 1989.

Cornell, Joseph. *Listening to Nature*. Nevada City, CA: Dawn Publications, 1987.

Elkington, John, Julia Hades, and Joel Makower. *The Green Consumer*. New York, NY: Penguin Books, 1990.

Finsh, Robert and John Elder, Eds. *Nature Writing*. New York, NY: W.W. Norton & Co., 1990.

Gore, Albert, Jr. *Earth in the Balance*. Boston, MA: Houghton Mifflin, 1992.

Gutnik, Martin J. *Ecology*. New York, NY: Franklin Watts, Inc., 1989.

MacEachern, Diane. *Save Our Planet*. New York, NY: Dell Publishing, 1990.

Munson, Richard. *Cousteau*. New York, NY: Paragon House, 1991.

Sisson, Edith. *Nature With Children of All Ages*. New York, NY: Prentice Hall, 1990.

Spurglon, Richard. *Ecology*. Tulsa, OK: Usborne Publishers, Ltd., 1989.

MAGAZINES

National Wildlife Magazine. National Wildlife Federation: Vienna, VA.

Horticulture: The Magazine of American Gardening. 98 Washington Street, Boston, MA.

Wilderness Magazine. Wilderness Society, Washington, D.C.

NEWSPAPERS

USA Today. 1000 Wilson Blvd., Arlington, VA 22229

OTHER SOURCES

Nature Scope News published by the National Wildlife Federation.

The Conservancy Yearbook published by The Conservancy, Inc., Naples, FL.